Algrove Publishing Limited
36 Mill Street, P.O. Box 1238
Almonte, Ontario, Canada K0A 1A0

Telephone: (613) 256-0350
Fax: (613) 256-0360
Email: sales@algrove.com

National Library of Canada Cataloguing in Publication

Nye, Alvan Crocker
Furniture designing and draughting / Alvan Crocker Nye.

(Classic reprint series)
Includes index.
Reprint of 2nd ed., originally published: New York : W.T. Comstock, 1907.
ISBN 1-894572-97-1

1. Furniture design. 2. Furniture making. I. Title. II. Series: Classic reprint series (Almonte, Ont.)

TS880.N93 2004 684'.04 C2003-906773-4

Printed in Canada
#1-2-04

PUBLISHER'S NOTE

As the subtitle states, these are notes on design, not a complete treatment of the subject, if such exists. The great value of Nye's work is that he addresses himself as much to furniture makers as to other designers. His work may not be exhaustive of the subject but it is exemplary for a tyro craftsman.

His greatest service is not just raising the questions that makers should ask of themselves but in offering a thinking framework for considering them.

The Pratt Institute continues to be as active in art, design, and architecture as it was in Nye's day.

Leonard G. Lee
Publisher
February 2004
Almonte, Ontario

CARVED LOUIS XVI. ARM CHAIR.

FURNITURE DESIGNING AND DRAUGHTING

NOTES ON

The Elementary Forms, Methods of Construction and Dimensions of Common Articles of Furniture

BY

ALVAN CROCKER NYE, PH.B.

INSTRUCTOR IN FURNITURE DESIGNING
PRATT INSTITUTE, BROOKLYN, NEW YORK CITY

SECOND EDITION

1907

CONTENTS

PREFACE

THIS book for the use of students, architects and others who at times find it desirable to make drawings for furniture, has been prepared from material collected during an experience of some years as a designer of furniture for several of the most important furniture-makers in New York City.

It is assumed that a knowledge of how projection and perspective drawings are made has been obtained, and that the general principles of design and ornamental forms are familiar to the reader. It describes methods of construction as far as they relate to draughtsman's work, but stops there, for it is not the intention to make this an instruction book for those who wish to become cabinet-makers. The "man at the bench" may, however, find the parts relating to designing of interest even though the practical details are already known, and seem to him incomplete because many mechanical matters that he realizes are necessary in making furniture are not mentioned.

Construction details that have been omitted were not thought essential to the draughtsman, and if known by him would be of no service in making the design or working drawing, as they would not appear on either.

New York City, 1900. A. C. N.

LIST OF PLATES

ILLUSTRATIONS IN THE TEXT

FURNITURE.

CHAPTER I.

Definitions, Classification, Etc.

FURNITURE designing is the art of delineating and ornamenting household effects so they become objects of beauty and pleasure as well as service. Furniture designing means giving thought and study to the proposed plan; the seeking for the best forms, sizes, proportions, materials, and workmanship to produce what is required. It may be necessary to make several attempts before success is attained, but the result will be the best individual effort. In this sense designed furniture should be useful, handsome, and well made of properly selected material used in an attractive way. Furniture may be made without any special study or thought, the result being mechanical, careless and lacking in artistic qualities. A mechanic may make something that is serviceable but extremely ugly, and without design. If, however, he has the personal quality that causes him to take pride in the appearance of his work combined with the knowledge of how to proceed to obtain the beautiful he will become a designer, for he will put his mind to his work, giving it a personality, independent of chance effects.

Furniture made without this thought and study brings to the mind at once the feeling that something is wanting. Either the lines indicate an indecision in the mind of the maker, or the methods employed in its construction show no desire to produce the best effect with the material.

Furniture can be divided into three classes, according to use.

First, DOMESTIC FURNITURE, including that for dwellings of every rank.

Second, CIVIL FURNITURE, that for public buildings and places of business.

Third, ECCLESIASTICAL FURNITURE, for churches.

Furniture may also be divided into two groups named for the methods of construction. The first, *Framework,* includes seats, tables, mirrors, screens, etc., and all articles not boxed in. The second, *Casework,* includes chests, bureaus, sideboards, desks, etc., and all articles which are cased (boxed) in by panel work or its equivalent.

The materials from which furniture is usually made are wood, metal and stone. The use of metal and stone need not be considered here, because these materials are employed for extraordinary furniture of a more or less fixed architectural character not strictly within the general accepted meaning of the word. The natural material is wood, which has many qualities to recommend it. It is abundant, easily obtained, and easily prepared in convenient form for use. It is of light weight so that objects made from it are not heavy enough to become inconvenient, and it is sufficiently strong to serve all practical purposes.

The ease with which it is worked into the forms desired, and the facility with which necessary repairs may be made are recommendations in its favor. In addition to these advantages, which may be called technical, there are the æsthetic and physical reasons why wood is superior to other materials. It is agreeable to the eye in its natural state, which furnishes a large variety of colors, but if these do not meet the requirements stains of any shade can be applied with ease. It also assumes, under proper conditions, a polish of a greater or less degree. There are no objectionable sensations experienced when it is touched by the hand, as it is not hard or harsh, nor is the temperature unpleasant.

The kind of wood used may have an influence on the character of the design. Some woods are of a coarse, open grain hardly adapted to small details or fine work. Such woods are oak and ash. They are well suited to large, heavy articles for severe usage, and of broadly executed design. Woods like mahogany, stainwood and maple are of a fine, close grain and admit of a more delicate treatment. Mouldings and carving in these woods may be smaller in detail than seems proper for those of a coarser grain. This feeling is quite well recognized by everyone, so that furniture for halls, libraries, etc., is often of the coarse woods, reserving those of finer grain for the living-room, parlors and bedrooms.

The character of the wood need not affect the quality of the design, as each variety may receive equal æsthetic treatment. The bold, coarse work may have just as much feeling expressed in the design as the more delicate. It is not the material used that is the most important consideration, but the form and proportion of the article, and the harmony of the design with the surroundings. It is the study of these conditions that gives opportunity for the designer to display his skill. He asks himself: Shall the article be square or oblong? Shall it be high or low in proportion to the width? Or if, as frequently is the case, one or two dimensions are given, what will be the best proportion for the other?

After the general proportion and form is determined, then the dimensions of the component parts are considered, and it may happen that these will be the only ones left for the designer, as the conditions of the problem sometimes fix all other sizes. By the component parts is understood (taking a table as an example) the relation of the size of the leg to the whole, the thickness of the top, and its projection; the depth of the frame, etc. Such questions must be answered for every article, and on the solution depends the quality of the design.

The stumbling block for beginners in design is the habit of thinking in feet and inches. One of the first questions usually asked by students is, how many inches wide shall this, or that, be made? There is a feeling that because it cannot be answered at once it is impossible to make the drawing correctly. It is not necessary, in most instances, to know the figure, as the dimension is dependent entirely on the sense of proportion and practicability. All dimensions fixed by common usage are known or given to the designer; the others should be determined by the knowledge obtained from experience and observation. As the designer becomes proficient he learns that within limits a square post of a given size may be used in certain places, but whether it will look better a little larger or a little smaller is determined by judgment.

The sizes of material found in stock need not interfere with the expressing of ideas that may occur. Lumber can be obtained of almost any size desired, and if it is not at hand the next largest dimension can readily be cut down, at the small expense for waste and labor, which in special work is hardly to be considered. It certainly is not advisable to spoil a good design in order to use material without cutting a little to waste.

A good piece of furniture must be adapted to the intended use, and it should not defy the laws of nature even in appearance. It is not sufficient for it to be strong, but it must appear so, that no thought of weakness may occur; nor ought it to appear unstable. It must be well constructed, otherwise it soon becomes broken or rickety; and when new, if carelessly made, there will be something about it to cause dissatisfaction. It ought to be pleasing to the eye, not only in design but in workmanship, and its form should express its purpose. Excessive ornamentation is to be avoided. It is better to have too little ornament than too much.

Construction has been placed second in these requirements for good furniture, believing that by following the laws of utility and construction natural and rational forms will be obtained. A designer should, then, have a little knowledge of the principles of construction, and in the following chapters the usual methods will be described as far as is necessary for the needs of a draughtsman.

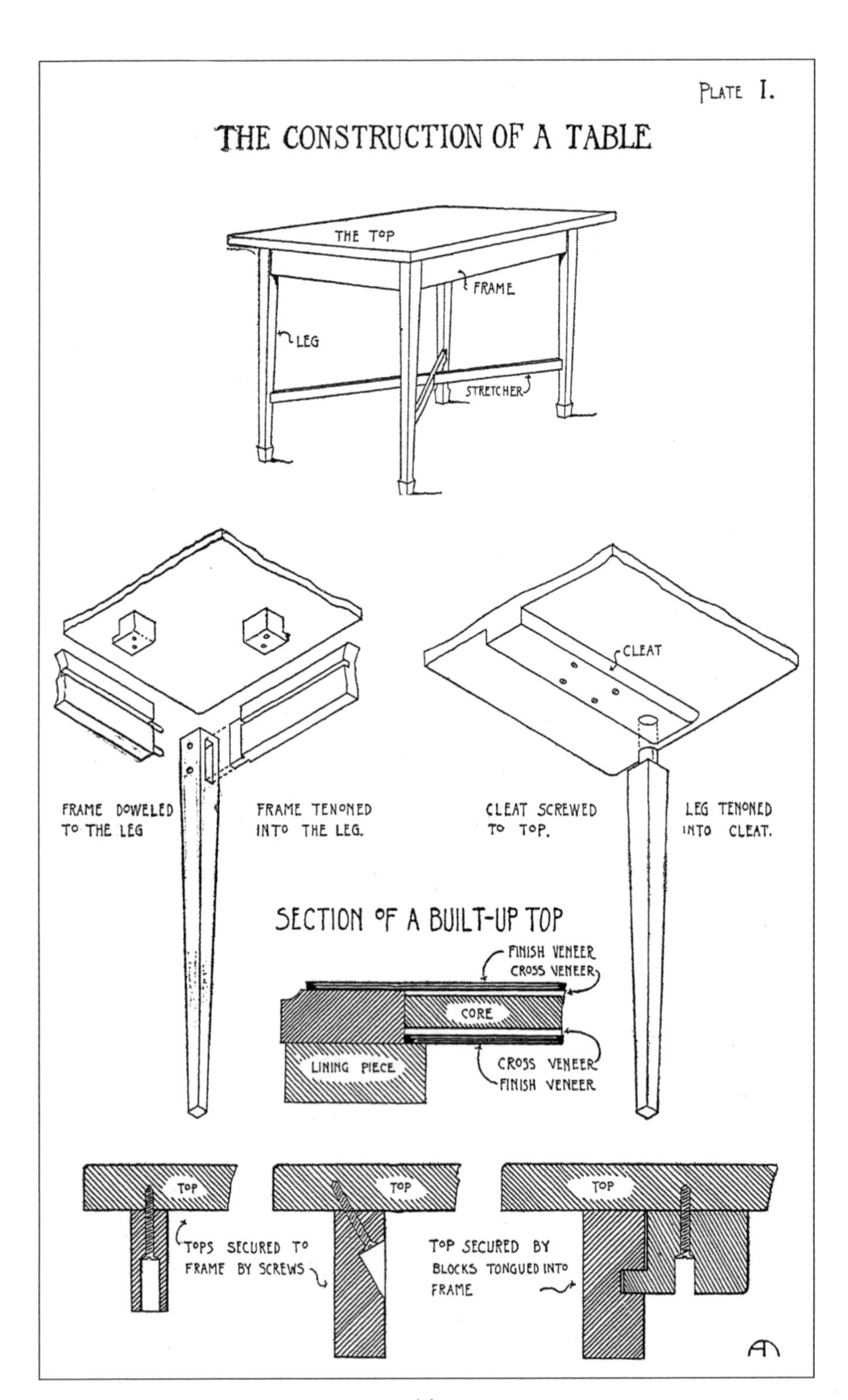
PLATE I.
THE CONSTRUCTION OF A TABLE
THE TOP
FRAME
LEG
STRETCHER
CLEAT
FRAME DOWELED TO THE LEG
FRAME TENONED INTO THE LEG.
CLEAT SCREWED TO TOP.
LEG TENONED INTO CLEAT.
SECTION OF A BUILT-UP TOP
FINISH VENEER
CROSS VENEER
CORE
LINING PIECE
CROSS VENEER
FINISH VENEER
TOP
TOP
TOP
TOPS SECURED TO FRAME BY SCREWS
TOP SECURED BY BLOCKS TONGUED INTO FRAME

CHAPTER II.

Tables.

THE table consists of a flat, level surface, suitable to receive whatever may be placed upon it, supported on one or more uprights. The word table properly applies to the top, which in early times was called a board, and it was, indeed, nothing more, the supports being trestles not attached in any way to the top itself. The top may be made of wood, marble, glass, etc., and is spoken of accordingly as a wooden table, marble table, glass table, etc. If the material is not mentioned, it may be supposed to be of wood. The name of the material is sometimes linked with the geometrical form of the top; thus, a square table, a circular marble table, an oval slate table, etc.

Tables are made high or low, according to the purpose for which they are used, and may be either with or without drawers. They are composed of three parts—the top, the frame and the legs. Plate I. The top has been described above. The frame is composed of horizontal rails immediately beneath the top and parallel with its edge. It is sometimes omitted on small tables, called "stands," but is common for the larger varieties. It serves as a means of binding the supports and top together as well as strengthening the top, which might otherwise sag beneath its load. The depth of frame gives apparent as well as real solidity to the whole structure. The legs are the supports for the table, and may be secured in several ways to the frame, or its equivalent. There may be but one leg, or post, directly under the center of the top, and ending at the floor in a spreading foot, thus forming a "pillar table." There may be two uprights, one at the middle of each end of a rectangular top, terminating in spreading feet, usually connected by a horizontal rail near the floor. There may be three, four or more legs, but four are most frequently used. These legs may be of an endless variety of shapes, and decorated by mouldings, carving, inlay, etc.

On Plate II. are shown twelve legs, which can be termed elementary forms, as nearly all others can be reduced to one of these. They are shown as chair legs, but they differ from table legs in proportions only. By comparing the plans and elevations, the drawings explain themselves clearly; but it is desirable to study particularly numbers 11 and 12. Eleven is the "bandy leg," with the ball and claw-foot used on "Dutch" and "Colonial" furniture. In many ways it resembles 12, which is the "Louis XV.," or "French bandy leg." This latter is much lighter, more graceful and ornamental than the Dutch form, but it at times seems too frail to support the weight it carries; and, again, the curved lines make it appear as if bending beneath the strain. In many of the exaggerated patterns of these legs the violent curvature causes the defects not only to become more prominent, but actually makes the leg weak. If the curvature is great, the vertical grain of the wood crosses it at one or more points, and at each of these places there is danger of the leg breaking. By examining the drawings Nos. 11 and 12 (a larger drawing of 12 in three positions is shown on Plate III.) it will be seen that a vertical line may be drawn throughout the entire length of the leg without intersecting its curved outline. This vertical line represents, then, a portion of the stick from which the leg is cut that has not had the strength weakened. The leg increases in strength directly in proportion as the distance between the contour lines and such a vertical widens. The draughtsman is to observe that, although moulded and cut in irregular forms, the cross-section of this leg at any place is practically square, and that in making it a square stick is first sawn so as to have the shape shown as front and side elevation, Plate III., and then turned over at right angles, on the vertical axis, and the same form cut again. As a result the diagonal view will curve as shown. When the leg is complete and casually examined it is seen in the diagonal view. It is with the recollection of such a view in mind that the designer too frequently lays out the curve for the front and side elevation, giving them the sharp sweep he really intends for the diagonal resultant curve. When the work is made from such a drawing the draughtsman is surprised to find how great the curve is. In designing the bandy leg the proper method is to draw its three elevations and plans as on Plate III. and study the outlines carefully till sure they are right.

Whatever may be the shape of table legs, they should be proportioned to the dimensions of the top, that they may not seem either too frail or stronger than necessary for the purpose of support.

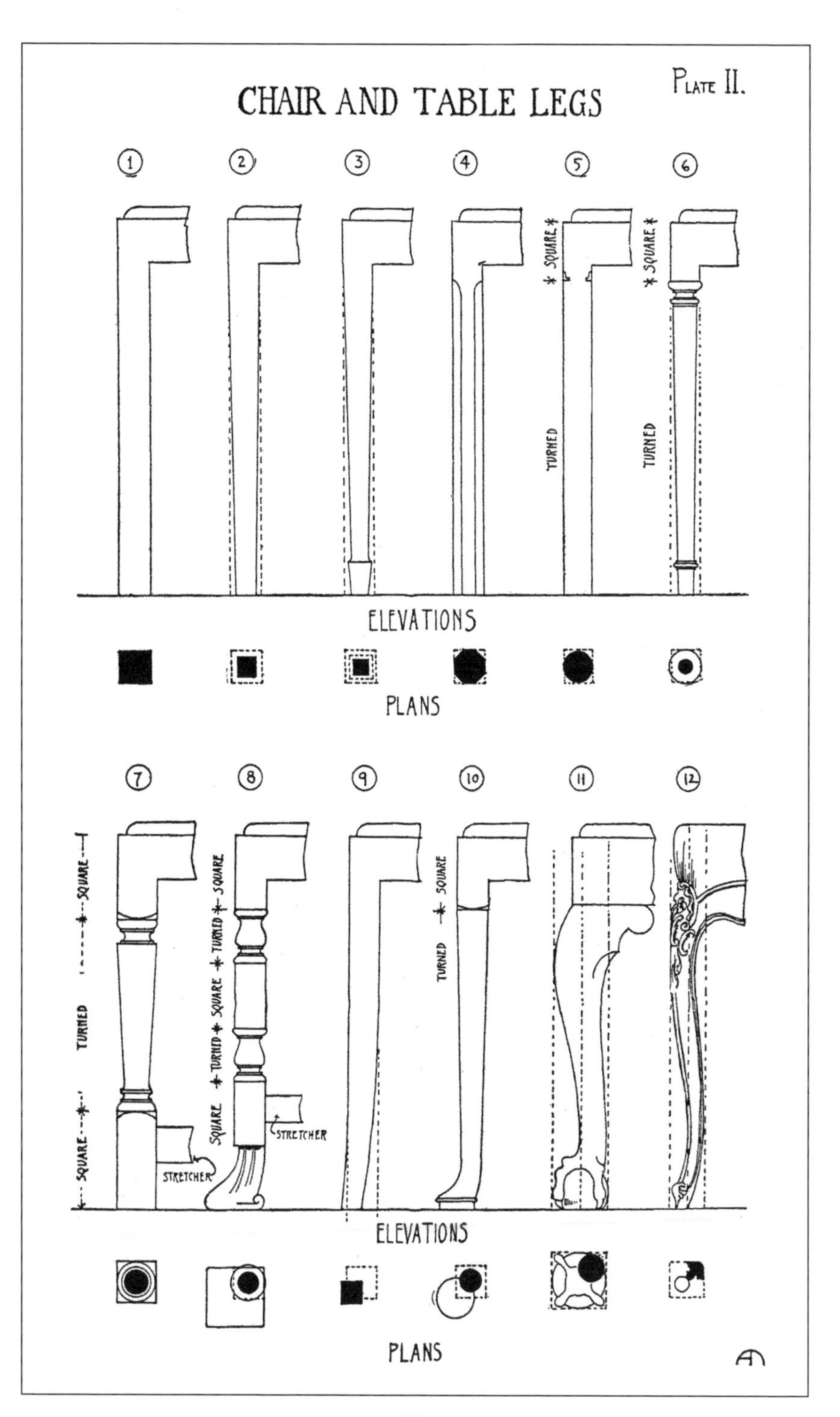
CHAIR AND TABLE LEGS
PLATE II.
1
2
3
4
5
6
SQUARE
TURNED
SQUARE
TURNED
ELEVATIONS
PLANS
7
8
9
10
11
12
SQUARE
TURNED
SQUARE
STRETCHER
SQUARE
TURNED
SQUARE
TURNED
SQUARE
STRETCHER
SQUARE
TURNED
ELEVATIONS
PLANS

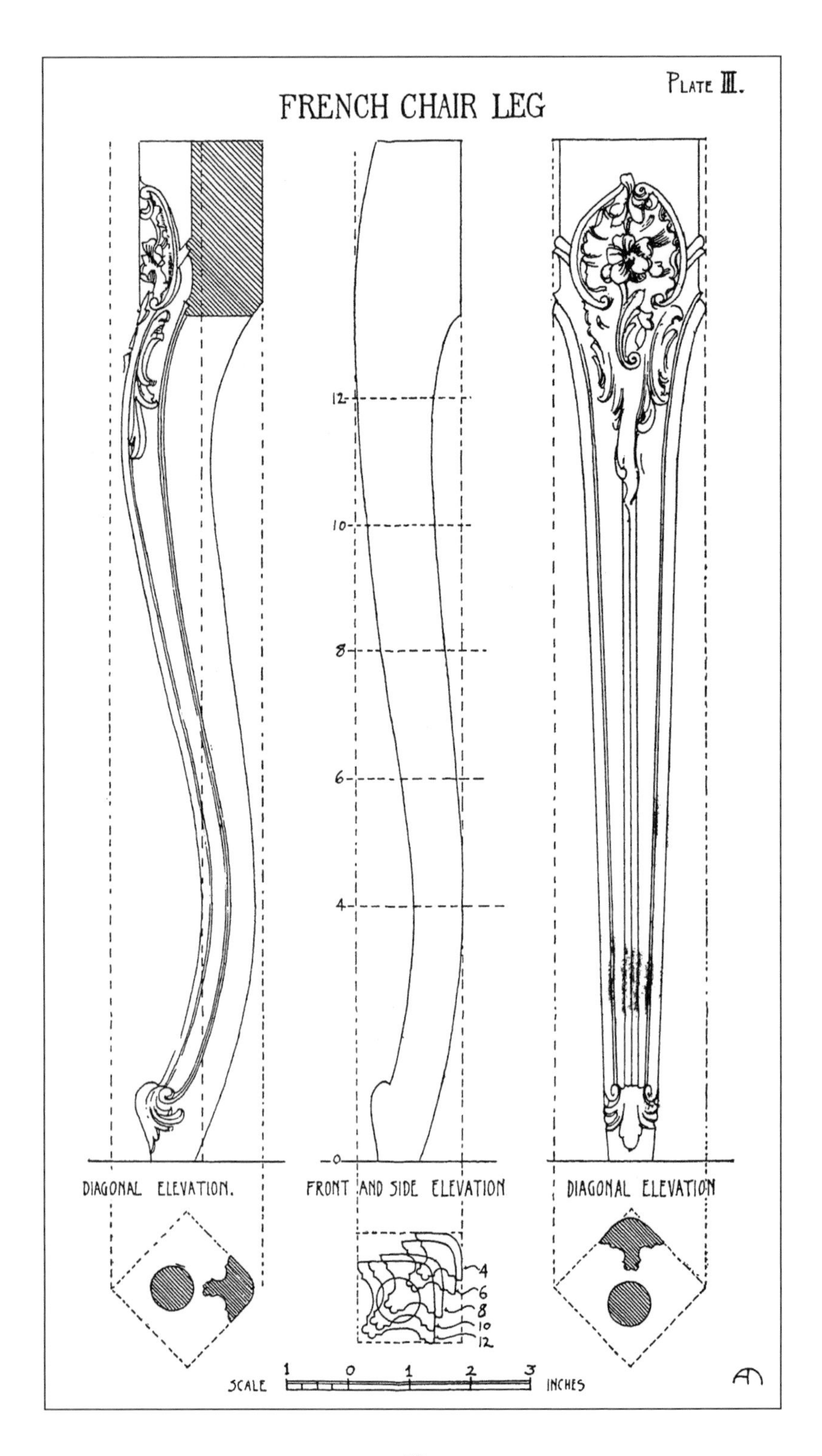
PLATE III.
FRENCH CHAIR LEG
12
10
8
6
4
0
DIAGONAL ELEVATION.
FRONT AND SIDE ELEVATION
DIAGONAL ELEVATION
4
6
8
10
12
SCALE
1 0 1 2 3
INCHES

Occasionally it may be desirable to make them so small and delicate that the table becomes shaky, owing to the elasticity of the wood, though they may be quite strong enough in appearance, and in reality to sustain the weight intended to be placed on them. When such is the case the legs can be connected, near the floor, by horizontal braces, known as stretchers. Plate VIII. shows three arrangements of stretchers as applied to chairs, and those for tables are similar. Stretchers are sometimes used for æsthetic reasons when

TURNINGS

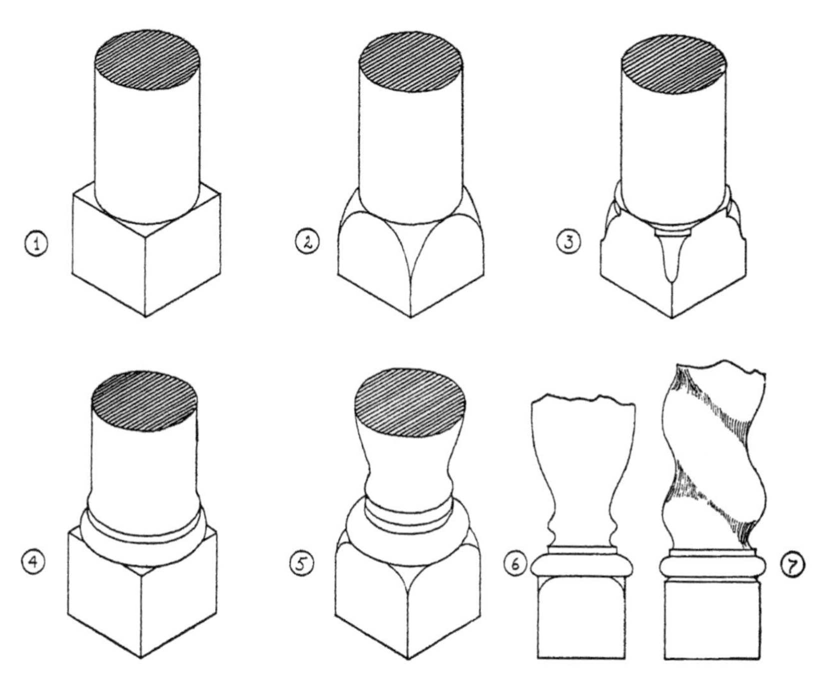

not needed to stiffen the support. Tables having legs like Nos. 7 and 8, Plate II., do not look well without stretchers; the baluster forms of the turnings and the heavy foot of each leg seeming to demand a framework binding the supports together.

Turnings are used continually in the construction of furniture, and they always appear smaller than a square stick of the same dimensions. This is apparent in the above illustrations. No. 1 shows the projection of the corner of a parallelopiped beyond the inscribed cylinder turned from it. The angular projection exists whenever an abrupt change from a square to a turned section is made. As this is objectionable in furniture work, it is cut away by rounding off the angle, as in No. 2, or by moulding it, as in No. 3. Nevertheless, if, as in these examples, the diameter of the cylinder and the side of the square are the same, the turning appears so much smaller than the square portion of the stick that the transition is too great.

When the design will admit, the square parts of the stick are cut down after the turning is made, so that they are a trifle smaller than the turned portions. This makes the two sections seem more nearly of the same dimensions, and is shown in No. 4, where a torus and fillet are also introduced to make the change of form more gradual. This same feature is shown in No. 5, where the angles of the square are cut away. The square is smaller than the diameter of the turning, and the torus is introduced to grade the transition. No. 6 is a longitudinal section of No. 5. The use of the torus or a bead between the square and turned parts of a post seems desirable in most cases, whatever the profile of the turning. No. 7 shows it in use on a twisted turning.

The depth of the frame of the table is largely a matter of individual taste. If, however, the table is one at which a person is to sit, with his knees beneath it, the frame must not be so deep as to reduce the space between its lower edge and the floor to less than two feet.

An important condition of beauty in a table is its stability. It should not appear insecure on its feet, as happens if the legs are placed too far beneath the top. A safe guide is not to make the spread of the feet of a table less than two-thirds the spread of the top; or, in other words, the overhang is one-sixth of the top. The overhang may be considerably more than this before the table becomes dangerously insecure, but it will have, nevertheless, an appearance of instability, especially if the width of the top is less than the height above the floor.

It is well to round off slightly the corners of rectangular tables, that they may not present a sharp angle.

The size of a table is determined by its use and the location it is to occupy. Unless intended for a special purpose it is thirty inches high.

Possibly the most important uses to which tables are put are those of dining and writing. For either of these a table thirty inches high can be and is used continually, but there are those who find this somewhat too high. A dining table should be sufficiently low that a person need not raise the elbows when cutting his food, and that his plate rests well below him. If a writing table is too high, it is tiresome to sit at and write. Many dining tables and writing tables are, therefore, made but twenty-nine inches high. The side table used in dining rooms as a place from which to serve dishes or to carve should be thirty-six inches high.

A dressing table is made thirty inches high, unless the person to use it requests that it be made otherwise. Parlor, fancy tables, etc., intended for ornamental use only, are made to correspond with the surroundings of the rooms in which they are placed, and may be any desired height, as they are neither intended to sit or stand at. The following list will give the dimensions of tables of average sizes that have been made and found satisfactory. It will serve as a guide or starting point in laying out new designs:

DIMENSIONS OF TABLES.

Variety.	Length.	Width.	Height.	Remarks.
Bedroom	31	22	29	
"	18	18	30	Commode.
Bijou	30	22	30	
Carving table	42	20	36	
Dressing table	36	20	30	
Extension table	66	66	30	Round.
" "	54	54	30	Square.
Library table	51	41	30	Oval.
" "	42	27	29	
" "	54	34	29	
" "	60	36	29	
Tea table	13	13	20	Round.
" "	18	18	24	
" "	23	23	18	Upper Shelf.
" "	30	17	29	Lower Shelf.

Note: All dimensions are in inches.

The parts of a table have already been named; it remains to see how they are put together.

The frame is joined to the legs either by the mortise and tenon or by doweling. The former joint was the old way of framing, but since the introduction of dowels the tenon has largely gone out of use among furniture makers. They consider it old-fashioned. And owing to the shrinkage of the tenon or the carelessness with which it is made, it does not seem as strong or equal to a dowel-joint.

The mortise and tenon consists of a tongue (tenon) cut on the end of one of the joined pieces so as to fit tightly in a cavity (mortise) sunk in the other piece. In table work the tenon is on the end of the frame, and may or may not be its full width, while the mortise is in the leg. Plate I.

The dowel joint derives its name from the dowel, a wooden pin, used for fastening the two pieces together by inserting part of its length in one piece, the rest of it entering a corresponding hole in the other. Where possible, more than one dowel is used. In table work two or more are fitted in holes bored for them in the end of the frame, and in the proper position on the legs are corresponding holes in which the dowels fit, and are glued when the two parts are brought together. Some small tables are constructed without a frame; in place of it there is a wooden cleat fastened to the underside of the top and the full diameter of the leg is inserted in this block; or if the leg is of large size it is tenoned into the block.

The top of a table may be solid or veneered. When small and cheap work is desired, it can be made of solid wood; but otherwise it should be built up and veneered. Solid wood tops shrink, crack, or warp. The only sure way of avoiding these unfortunate occurrences is to "build-up" the top. The building up process consists in constructing a core of some common, well-dried, lifeless wood, preferably chestnut or pine. This core is of several strips of wood doweled together at the edges until a board is made about the size of the required top. These strips are arranged in a way that the annular rings curve in opposite directions in each alternate piece. The core is next cross-veneered on *both* sides with hardwood, generally oak. A cross-veneering is laid so that the grain is at right angles to that of the wood on which it is applied. In table work it is at right angles to the grain of the core and the finish veneer; both of these naturally follow the length of the top. All around the edge of the top, after it is cross-veneered, is fastened a strip of the finish wood of the table (Plate I.) Finally, *both* sides are again veneered with the finish wood; that is, if the wood is not too expensive. If it is costly, a cheaper veneer is placed on the underside.

When the design calls for the edge of the top to appear thick, it is a needless waste of material to construct it of wood the full thickness, besides making an unnecessarily heavy piece of furniture. To avoid this and yet obtain the appearance wanted, a frame of wood is fastened to the underside of the otherwise thin top, giving the thickness required. This frame is called the lining piece, and the top is said to be lined up.

The method of fastening the top to the frame of the table varies with the class of work and the size. If it is a small table, no special care is taken, the fastening consisting of screws driven through the

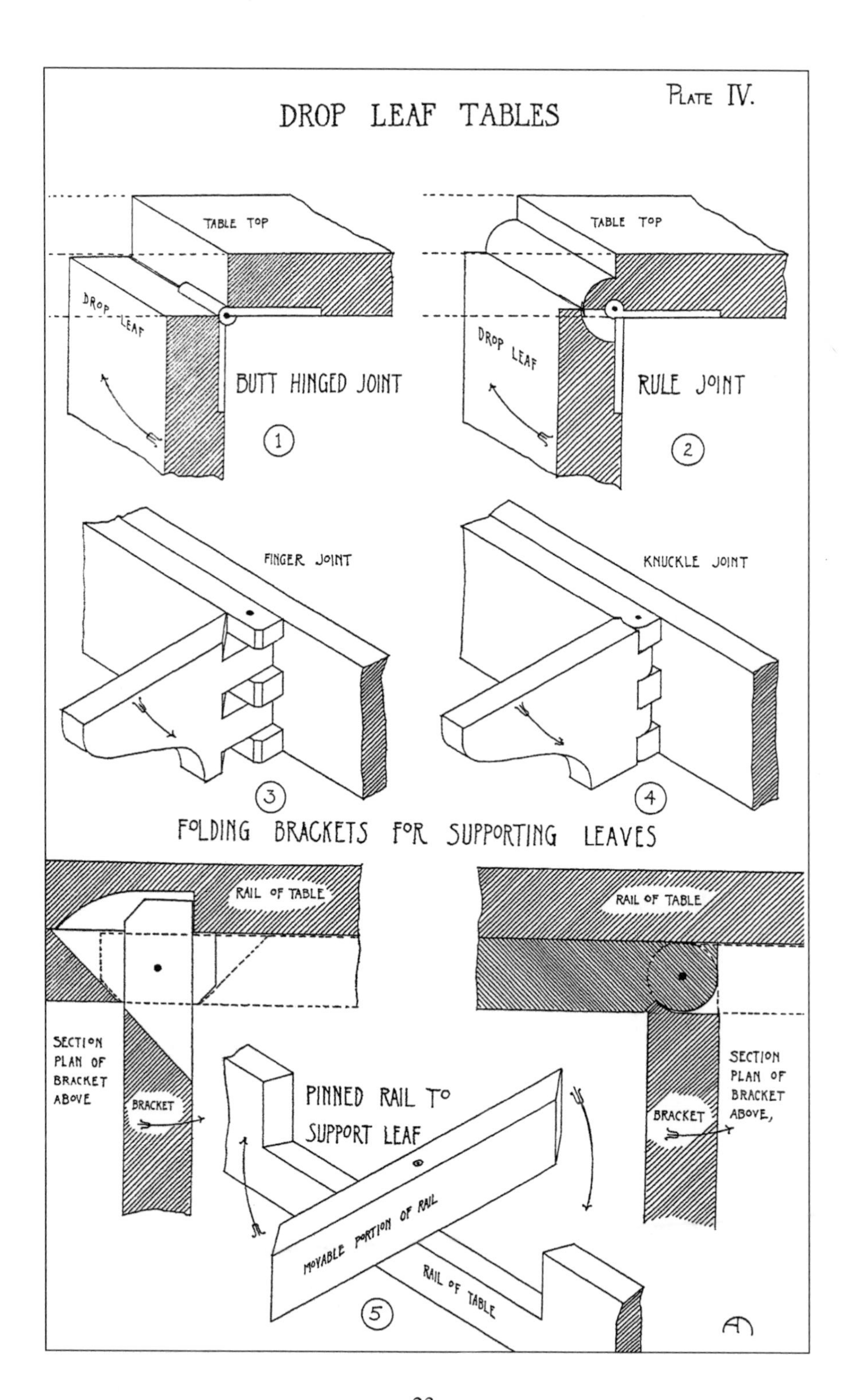
PLATE IV.
DROP LEAF TABLES
TABLE TOP
DROP LEAF
BUTT HINGED JOINT
1
TABLE TOP
DROP LEAF
RULE JOINT
2
FINGER JOINT
3
KNUCKLE JOINT
4
FOLDING BRACKETS FOR SUPPORTING LEAVES
RAIL OF TABLE
SECTION PLAN OF BRACKET ABOVE
BRACKET
PINNED RAIL TO SUPPORT LEAF
MOVABLE PORTION OF RAIL
RAIL OF TABLE
5
RAIL OF TABLE
SECTION PLAN OF BRACKET ABOVE,
BRACKET

rail into the underside of the top. If the rail is narrow and thick enough, the screw is set straight through it. If, however, it is a wide rail, the screws are driven in recesses cut for them on the inner side. Most tables are too large to admit of this method. A top fastened as just described is held fast to the frame, so if shrinkage takes place there is a strain somewhere that may result in a cracked top. To allow for any movement that may occur, short blocks having a tongue that fits securely in a groove cut on the inner side of the table frame are screwed to the underside of the top. These blocks hold the top firmly in position, and yet if a shrinkage takes place they are free to move in the grooved frame.

Tables are frequently provided with a drawer either in the frame or hung beneath the top on cleats. How drawers are made, and the different kinds, are described in Chapter V.

There are occasions that require a table larger than it is convenient to keep standing continually in a room. In early times, when tables were nothing more than boards resting on trestles, if they were not needed the board was turned up against the wall and the trestles stowed away. When the top and the supports became fastened together, methods were invented for reducing the size of the table, that it might not take up too much space, or for enlarging it for special purposes. One of these methods is the use of leaves or flaps that fold down against the side of the legs. Two things are to be observed in such tables—the way the leaves are hinged, and how they are supported when raised.

In cheap work the edges of the leaves and top, where they meet. are cut straight and square, forming a plain joint, and the leaf is hung with a hinge on the underside. Plate IV., No. 1. When hung in this way a small crack is seen between the top and the leaf as the latter hangs down, and the hinge also shows.

In better work both these things are considered faults, and to avoid them the *rule joint* is used. Plate IV., No. 2. This joint is made by moulding both the edge of the leaf and the top where they meet, the moulding on the leaf being the reverse of that on the top. The top is cut with a projecting tongue, rounded like a quarter cylinder, and the leaf is hollowed to receive it. The hinges are sunk into the underside of the top and leaf, with their center corresponding with the center of the quarter round moulding of the meeting edges. Then, as the leaf swings up or down its rebated edge fits snugly against the moulded edge of the top. The hinge is practically concealed and there is no open joint.

There are small tables made with two leaves hinged in a similar way to that just described, so when both are down the table is no wider than the cylinder plus the thickness of the leaves.

Leaves may be supported by brackets attached to the frame and swinging out under them. The brackets may be hung with metal hinges, but better ways are illustrated on Plate IV., Nos. 3 and 4. These drawings show folding brackets somewhat similar in construction made by fastening to the side rail of the table frame a block with one end cut so as to interlock with one end of the bracket. A metal pin through the two pieces where they interlock serves as an axis on which the bracket turns. In No. 3, the finger joint, the corners of the working parts are beveled off, that the bracket may turn. In No. 4, the knuckle joint, they are rounded so the parts fit clearly and are in contact in whatever position the bracket may be. The finger joint can be made the strongest, as more wood may be left between the pin axis and the ends of the tonges than in the other. The knuckle joint is considered the neatest, but it is more difficult to construct, and as the bracket is hidden from view the difference in appearance does not warrant its use.

Sometimes, when the depth of the frame will permit, a portion of it may be cut so as to swing on a pin at the middle, and, thus, when turned at right angles to the frame, one half is beneath the top, the rest acting as a support for the leaf. Plate IV., No. 5.

Bracket supports are not strong, and a table with a large leaf is unstable. To obviate this, tables are made with a leg that swings out under the leaf, giving it support, and stability to the table. When such a table has a stretcher, the movable leg is strengthened by fastening it to a hinged bracket at the stretcher level, in addition to the one on the frame. Another way of supporting drop leaves is to arrange slides that may be pulled out from the table frame beneath the leaves when they are raised.

The tables described thus far have the top fixed, but there are those with the tops pivoted, so when they are turned about the pivot a quarter way round the leaves will be supported by the frame of the table, which in the revolved position of the top lies beneath them. Two varieties of this style are illustrated on Plate V. The first is an old-style drop-leaf table pivoted at the middle of the top. By raising both leaves and turning the top on its pivot the ends of the frame are brought beneath the leaves to support them. The second table is in more common use. The top is of two parts, of the same size and shape, hinged together so one part folds over on the other. When

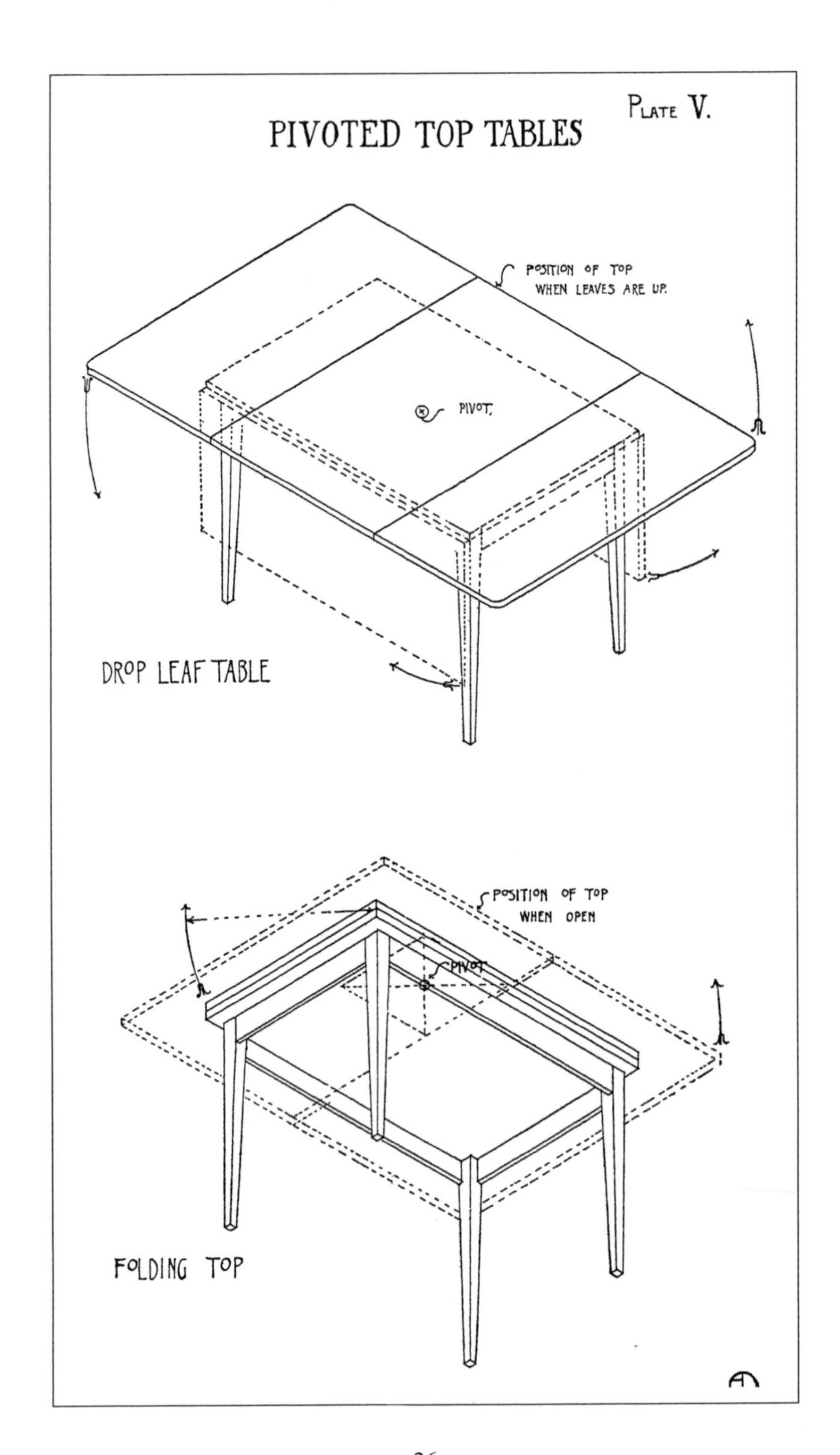
PLATE V.
PIVOTED TOP TABLES
POSITION OF TOP
WHEN LEAVES ARE UP.
PIVOT.
DROP LEAF TABLE
POSITION OF TOP
WHEN OPEN
PIVOT
FOLDING TOP

folded the top is but half the size it is when open, and can be turned on the pivot to a position over one end of the frame with the hinged edge directly across the middle. The upper leaf may then be unfolded and will rest on the other end of the frame. Such tables are usually square when open, and are spoken of as card tables.

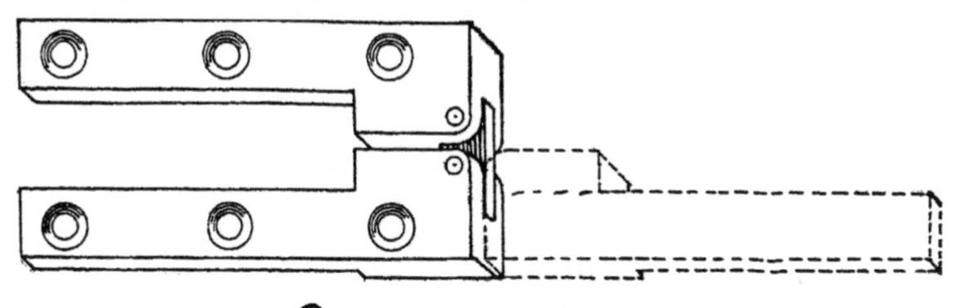

CARD-TABLE HINGE.

The hinges used for joining the two parts of the top are not ordinary butts. They are of a special form, as will be seen from the adjoining illustration, and are placed at each end of the leaves, with the screws driven into the edges. This avoids the appearance of any objectionable metal work on the surface of the table top, as would be the case if ordinary butts were used with their entire flaps exposed to view. The card table hinge has no projecting knuckle above the surface of the table, as its parts, instead of turning on a single pin, are joined by a link turning on a pin in each flap of the hinge. This link is flush with the edge of the table when the leaves are closed, and flush with the top when they are open. There are other forms of this hinge available.

Other ways of increasing the size of tables are shown on Plate VI. These are extension tables.

The upper one is the old "draw table," and is not used much now. A study of the drawings will show that the leaves enlarging the table are slides that pull out from beneath the top. Each slide is about half the length of the top, so the table is nearly doubled in length when both are pulled out. It should be noted, too, that to be of service the slide must be pulled out its full length; otherwise the top and slide are not on the same level. This means that there are but two changes in size for this kind of a table. Either it is increased by the whole of one leaf or by both. The top of the table is not solidly fastened to the frame, but is free to move vertically a little, though prevented from moving in any other direction by keys fastened to its underside and passing through a rail the same thickness as the leaves, fastened to the frame. Each side has two bearing pieces fastened to its underside, one at each end. The bearing pieces are as long as the frame of the table, or a little longer, and when the slide is drawn out one end of them bears against the underside of the rail to which the top is keyed, while their lower edge rests on the frame of the table, notched to receive it. They are cut at the proper level, so when drawn out the top and slide are on a level, and the slide is held securely in place against the edge of the top.

The common extension table is familiar to everyone. The illustration presents it in the simplest form. It is really a table with a telescopic frame, and provided with extra sections of a top that may be added till the frame is extended its full length. The leaves are made of sizes from twelve inches to twenty wide, and the tables are made to extend as desired, the average being from twelve to sixteen feet.

Each manufacturer has his own method of constructing the telescopic frame, or slides, as they are called, the differences depending on patented devices for holding the slides together. The principle, however, is the same in all. Plate VI. illustrates a section through two slides, showing one device. The sides of the slides are grooved to receive keys that dovetail them together. Each slide, when pulled out to the extreme, laps over those adjoining it about one-third, and stops are provided to prevent their being separated more than this. The slides are of wood, an inch and a half to two inches thick, nearly as wide as the table frame is deep and about as long as the underside of the table when closed will permit. The number of slides depends on the length to which the table is to be extended. There are two sets—an odd number on each side of the table. The outer pair are screwed firmly to the underside of one-half of the top, and the inner pair to the other half. All the slides except these are free to move. As most tables extend too much for the slides to support the weight at the middle, it is usual to provide a center leg. This leg is fastened to the middle of a transverse rail screwed securely to the middle slide of each group.

The frame of the table, when extended, is separated at the middle, and if the cloth cover is not used the slides are exposed to view. This interrupted frame is unsightly, and each leaf may be provided with its section of frame, so that when in place no gap is left between the extended ends. There are card tables made so two of the legs and one side can be pulled out to support a leaf when it is open. They are small extension tables, the frame itself forming a part of the slides.

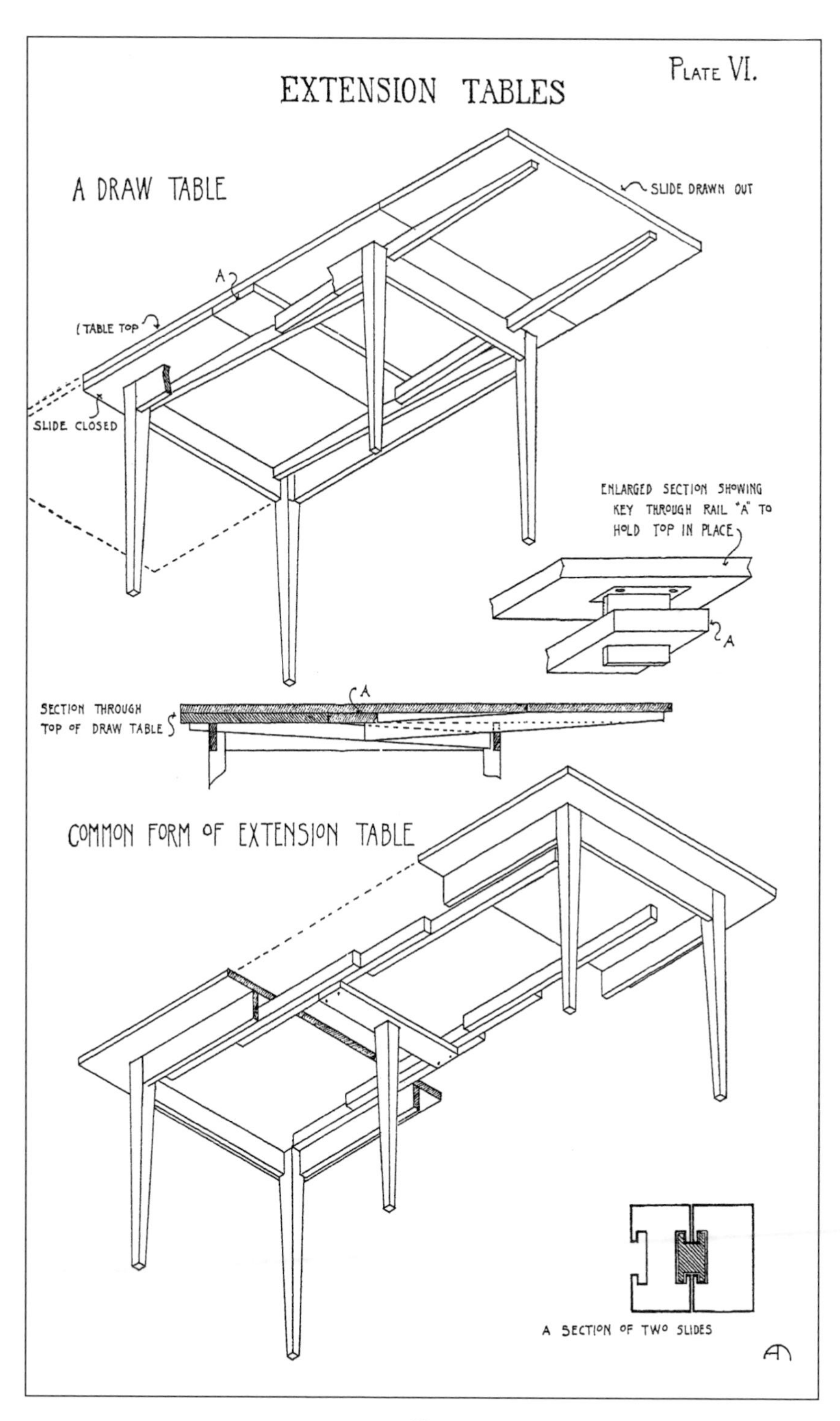
EXTENSION TABLES
PLATE VI.
A DRAW TABLE
SLIDE DRAWN OUT
A
TABLE TOP
SLIDE CLOSED
ENLARGED SECTION SHOWING
KEY THROUGH RAIL "A" TO
HOLD TOP IN PLACE
A
SECTION THROUGH
TOP OF DRAW TABLE
A
COMMON FORM OF EXTENSION TABLE
A SECTION OF TWO SLIDES

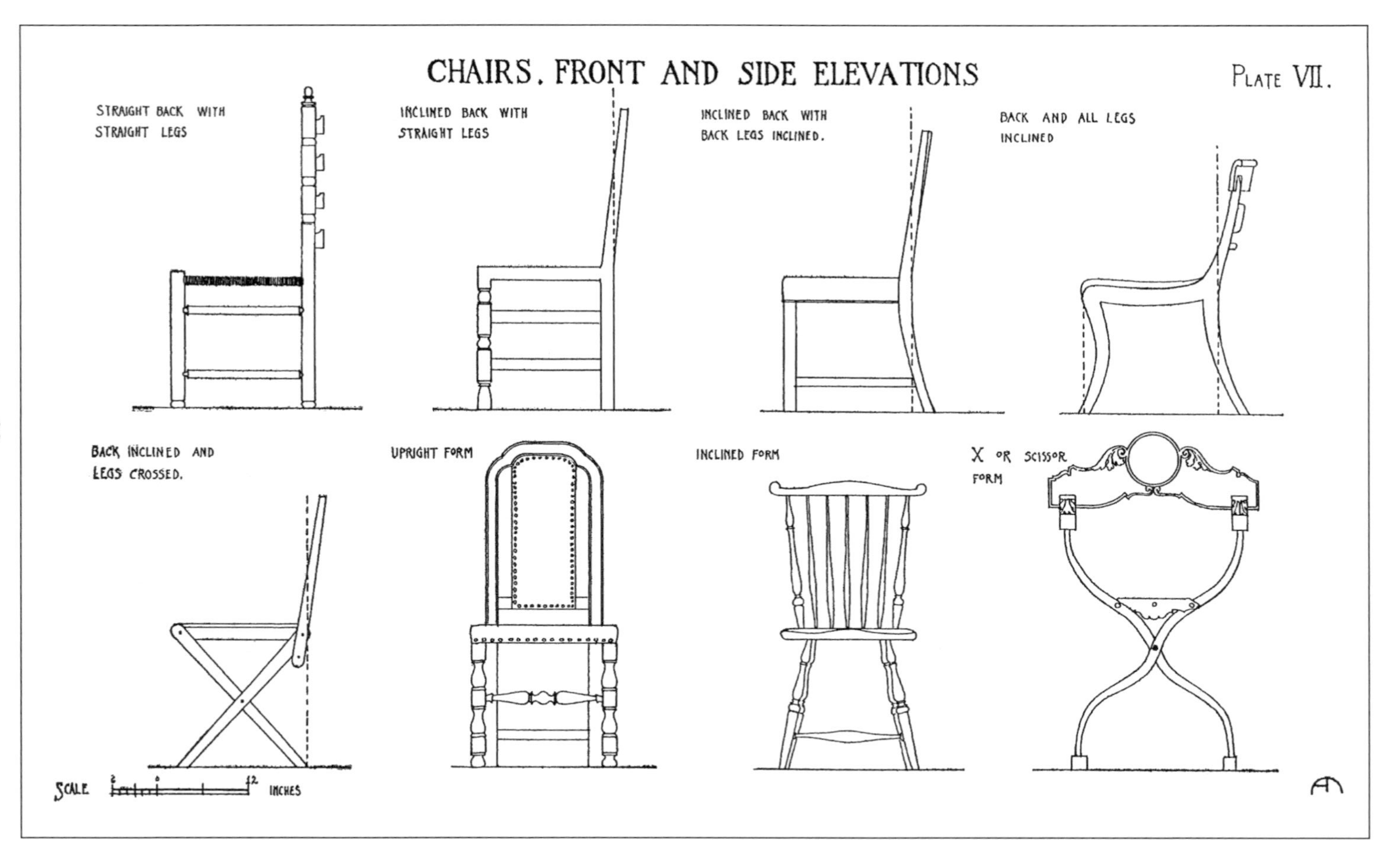
CHAIRS. FRONT AND SIDE ELEVATIONS
PLATE VII.
STRAIGHT BACK WITH
STRAIGHT LEGS
INCLINED BACK WITH
STRAIGHT LEGS
INCLINED BACK WITH
BACK LEGS INCLINED.
BACK AND ALL LEGS
INCLINED
BACK INCLINED AND
LEGS CROSSED.
UPRIGHT FORM
INCLINED FORM
X OR SCISSOR
FORM
SCALE
2
0
12
INCHES

CHAPTER III.

Chairs, Seats, Sofas.

THE parts of a chair are the legs, the seat frame, the back, and the arms. Plate XI.

The seat frame, and in most instances all the rails, are doweled to the legs and back posts. The seat frame is stiffened by corner blocks screwed securely to the inner side. If these blocks are wide and well fastened, they add very materially to the strength of the chair. The upholstery blocks mentioned on page 31 also stiffen the framing. The conditions given the designer usually determine the use of the chair and how much of it is to be upholstered. With this information given, he is free to make the rest as he likes, and he decides upon the form and proportion of the chair as a whole without respect to detail. This may be studied in plan and elevation at a convenient scale, or perhaps in perspective, if the idea is sufficiently clear in the mind to do so. It is, however, only by means of the projection drawings that the true forms of the different parts may be known, and even though the sketch is made at once without their aid a knowledge of what they are like is necessary. Chairs, when drawn in side elevation, assume one of the five elementary forms shown on Plate VII., where attention is called to the relation of the supporting members to a vertical line. These outlines are drawn from actual examples, and are at the same scale for purposes of comparison.

The front elevation will appear like one of the three types shown on this plate. The one on the right, if drawn in side elevation, would have a straight back and straight legs; the one on the left would have the side elevation, like one of the first three illustrated; the one in the middle would appear in side elevation much the same as it does in the front, i. e., all legs and the back inclined. It is a drawing of a Windsor chair, with a solid wood seat, sometimes called the saddle seat, because of its shape. The legs and back posts are fastened in this seat by inserting the full size of the turning in holes bored for them, and the seat frame is omitted; but the legs are tied together by stretchers.

Italian and German chairs, with backs and legs of solid boards elaborately carved, appear in the same inclined form when drawn in elevation. The "scissor" pattern was originally a folding chair, but although the form is retained it is not always made to fold, though both folding and fixed chairs present a similar elevation. The plan of a chair seat approximates a square, a triangle, or a circle. The principal varieties, with the position of the legs in relation to the frame indicated by the shading, are shown on Plate VIII. The square plan, though not uncommon, is less frequently seen than the trapezoidal. This latter is perhaps the most used, either with the straight frame, as on the left of the dotted line in the illustration, or curved, as on the right. Triangular seats, though used in olden times, are not common now, except for corner seats.

The circular and composite plans are constantly employed. The composite form, made up of curves and marked "French," is the plan of the Louis XV. arm-chair, given as an example of rendering (Plate XVIII.), and the plan on the right marked "Windsor" is that of a Windsor chair, similar to the "inclined form" (Plate VII.).

The outline of nearly all chair backs is either rectangular or trapezoidal (Plate IX.). If of the first, the back posts are perpendicular to the floor line, and the legs are the same distance apart at the floor as at the seat level.

If of the second form, the back posts are inclined to the floor line so that the legs are nearer together at the floor than at the seat level, and the back of the chair is proportionately wider at the top than it is at the seat. Though a chair may have a more complex and elaborate back than any of those taken as examples for illustration, an analysis of the outline will result in finding that it is based on one of these figures. The other four shapes illustrated are not as frequently used as the first two. This is particularly true of the polygonal and semicircular patterns.

Both of these are taken from French examples. The elliptical back is also a favorite form for French chairs. The shield-back is characteristic of chairs made by Hepplewhite about 1793, and called by many "Colonial." It is well to observe, while studying these outlines, a constructive principle common to all of them. Whatever the outline of the back it is made up of two vertical posts extending from the floor to a horizontal rail connecting them at the top; at the

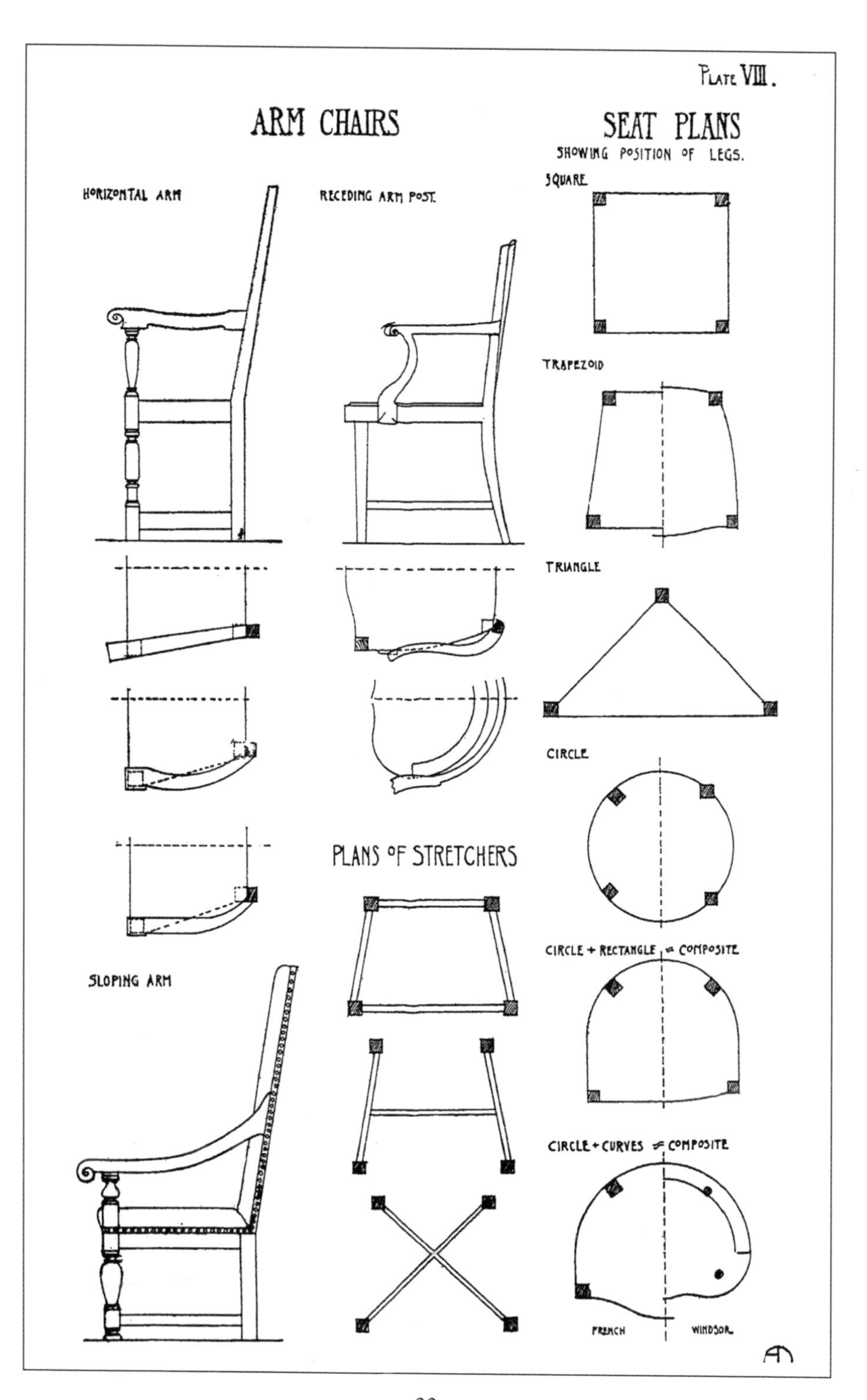
PLATE VIII.
ARM CHAIRS
SEAT PLANS
SHOWING POSITION OF LEGS.
HORIZONTAL ARM
RECEDING ARM POST.
SQUARE
TRAPEZOID
TRIANGLE
CIRCLE
PLANS OF STRETCHERS
CIRCLE + RECTANGLE = COMPOSITE
SLOPING ARM
CIRCLE + CURVES = COMPOSITE
FRENCH
WINDSOR

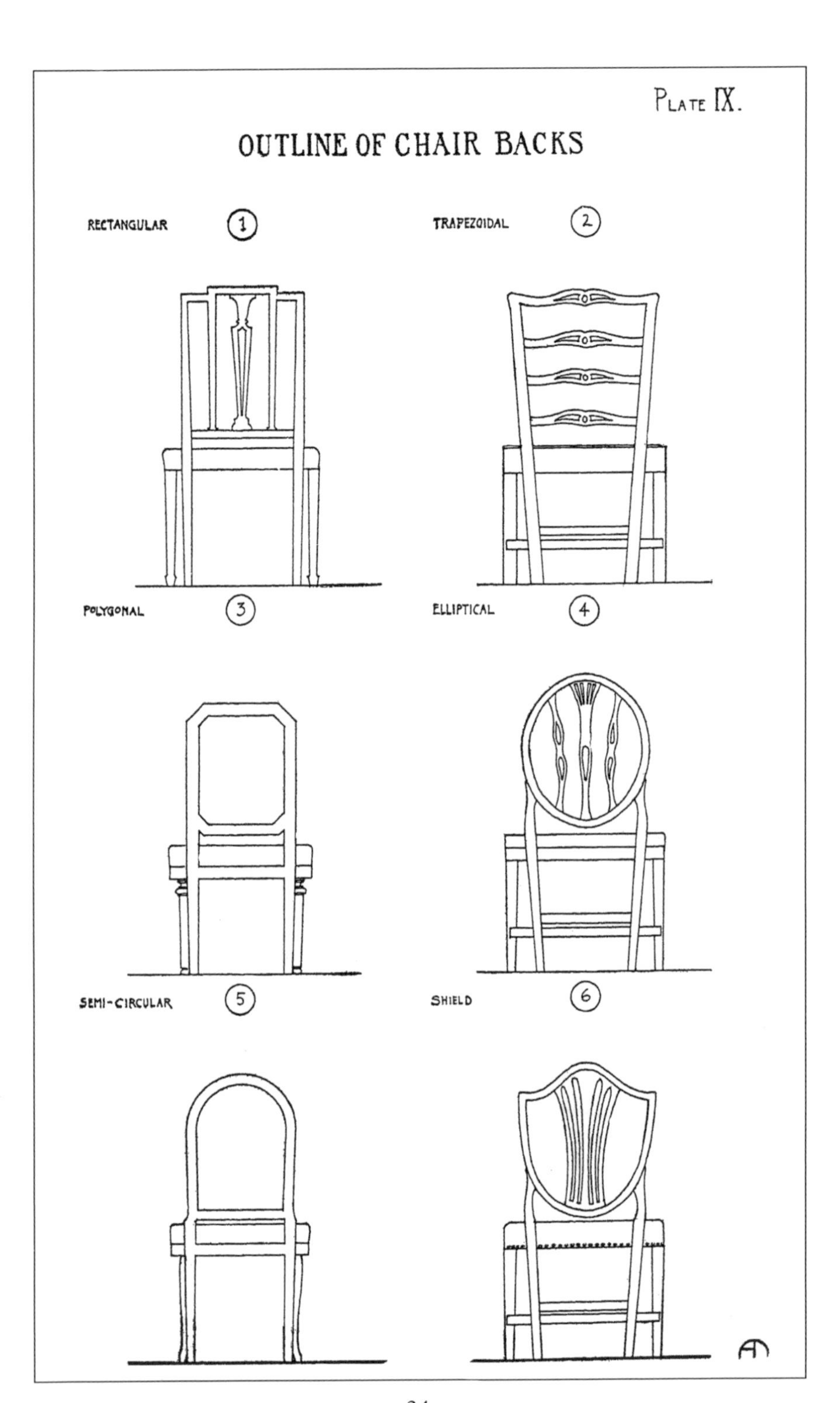
PLATE IX.
OUTLINE OF CHAIR BACKS
RECTANGULAR
1
TRAPEZOIDAL
2
POLYGONAL
3
ELLIPTICAL
4
SEMI-CIRCULAR
5
SHIELD
6

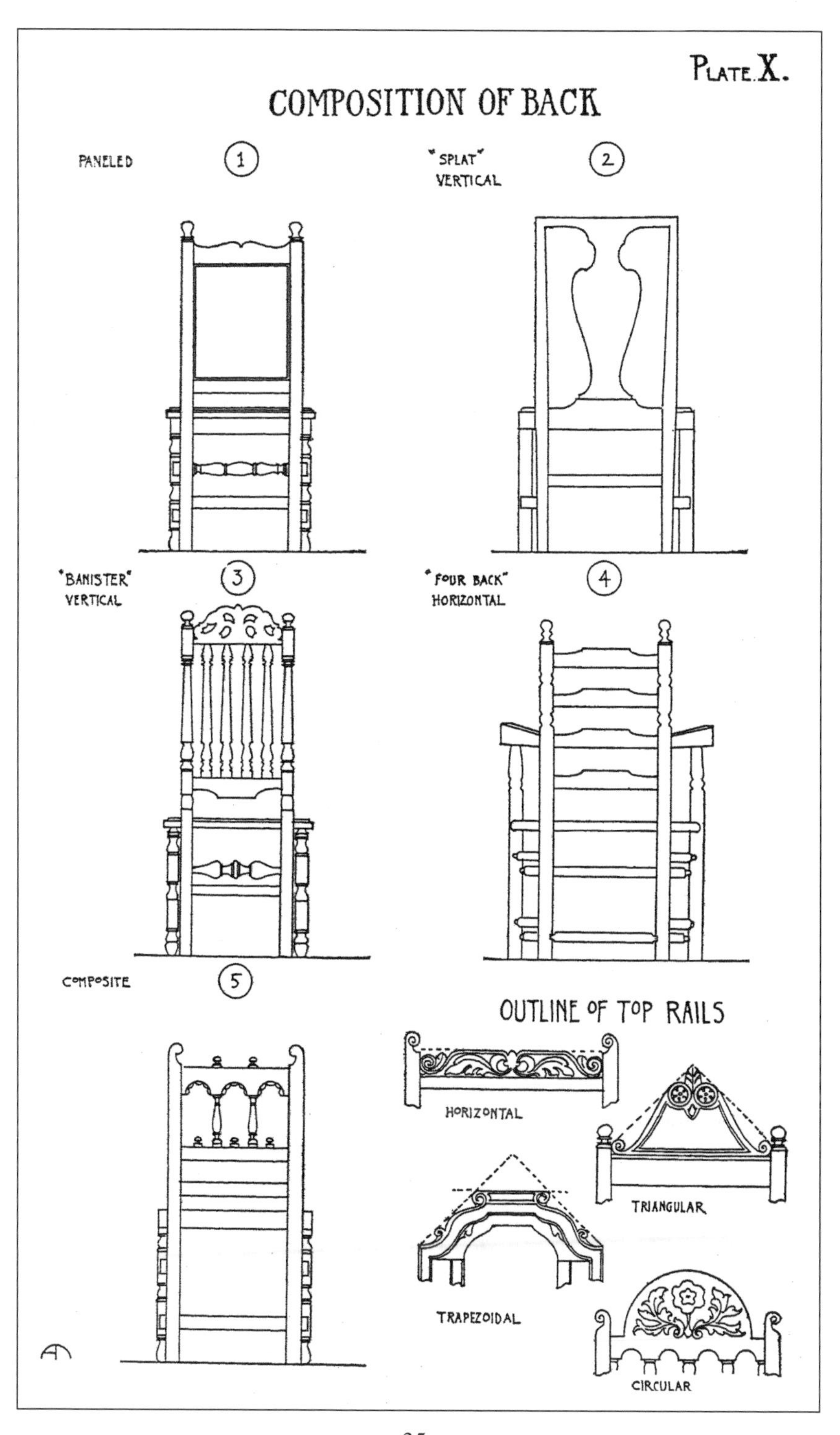
PLATE X.
COMPOSITION OF BACK
PANELED
1
"SPLAT"
VERTICAL
2
"BANISTER"
VERTICAL
3
"FOUR BACK"
HORIZONTAL
4
COMPOSITE
5
OUTLINE OF TOP RAILS
HORIZONTAL
TRIANGULAR
TRAPEZOIDAL
CIRCULAR

seat level is a horizontal rail (seat frame); and in some instances there is another horizontal rail at a greater or less distance above the seat.

The student is to notice especially that the uprights (the back legs) are of one piece from the floor to the top rail of the back. This is often forgotten by beginners in chair designing, and weak, almost impossible, shapes are given to the back as a result. The elliptical and shield-backs, though at first glance violating this rule, are really composed of the parts as mentioned above. A larger drawing of the shield-back, though at first glance violating this rule, are really composed of the parts as mentioned above. A larger drawing of the shield-back is given on Plate XVII., showing by the dotted lines the prolongation of the lower part of the leg; and the joints where the top and bottom rails of the shield meet the uprights are also indicated. Another chair back is also shown on the plate illustrating the same principle. There is but one exception to the above method of construction, and that is, when a solid wood seat is used; similar to the saddle seated Windsor; the German *Stuhle,* with turned legs; and the Italian *Scabelum,* with its solid board supports. In this case the legs and the back are separate. Each leg is inserted in holes for the purpose in the board seat.

Having determined on the outline of a chair back it is necessary to study its composition, that is, to decide how the space within the outline is to be treated. This question is sometimes decided before the design is begun, as, for instance, when it is panelled, or upholstered. If, however, it is to be of some other pattern, study is necessary. Aside from the methods just mentioned, the back may be filled with slats arranged in one of the four ways shown on Plate X.

A single broad slat ("splat") may be placed in the middle of the back between the top and the seat rail, or it may stop on a horizontal rail just above the seat. Such a slat can be treated as desired either with figured veneers, inlay, painting, carving, perforations, etc. A back composed of a number of vertical turned or half turned slats filling the space has been called a "banister back." But the slats are not always turned, they are sometimes flat, moulded, perforated, inlaid or carved. They are sometimes placed horizontally and bowed, the concave side toward the seat. The curvature increases as the slats approach the top; so, though the lower slat may be nearly straight, the top one is hollowed considerably to receive the shoulders of a person sitting in the chair. This gradual change in the curvature of the slats is sometimes substituted for the sloping of the back posts.

Chairs made with turned posts and having horizontal slats in the back were named by the number of slats. As, three backed, or four backed chairs; that is, three or four horizontal slats. Five backed chairs were quite uncommon.

It is perhaps almost unnecessary to say that both horizontal and vertical slats may be used in the same back. There is an endless variety of ways in which these slats and balusters may be grouped, spaced, and proportioned to fill the space well. Whether the slats or the spaces shall be the broadest? What is the best outline for the balusters? Are the kind of questions the designer is to ask himself, striving always to obtain the beautiful rather than the eccentric and curious forms.

The outline of the top rail of the "rectangular" and "trapezoidal" backs has its influence on the appearance of the chair, and it may be more or less ornamented. Four forms are shown on Plate X. which explain themselves.

In Plate VIII. are shown five plans of arm chairs. One of these has the arm straight, following the plan of the seat. Two of the others indicate how the space between the arms is made wider than the seat at the back by curving the arm; the front post remaining in the same position as in the first plan. The plans drawn beneath the chair with the "receding arm post" show how the arm may be a compound curve or a continuation of the curve of the back. In the former not only does the curve give a maximum width between the arms, but it also permits of the front scroll of the arm turning out, thus preventing the chair from seeming narrow.

In some chairs the plan of the arm follows the curve of the back so there is no angle where the two join. This is illustrated in the plan of a "Windsor" chair, where the piece from which the arm is cut is continuous from one side of the chair to the other, the slats of the back passing directly through it.

Chair arms may be horizontal or they may slope to a greater or less degree with the highest point where they join the back. Stretchers are used to strengthen the chair. The legs when braced by them are more firm and less likely to loosen at the seat frame joint. Plate VIII. gives the plans of three arrangements of stretchers. When placed high enough to be out of the way of the feet of a person using the chair the stretcher may form a trapezoid parallel to the seat frame; or if the chair seat is high and a foot rest is desired the stretcher may be arranged this way and set low for the purpose. In olden times European chairs were always made high and with a foot rest, that a person might keep his feet off of the cold floors. Now that it is not necessary to keep the feet away from the floor, it is not customary to allow them to touch the stretchers of chairs. These are, therefore, arranged diagonally between the legs of the chair; or, the front and back legs are joined together by rails, while a third unites the two side rails. This third rail may be set in any position, but frequently it is a little nearer the front than the back.

One of the most difficult tasks the furniture draughtsman has is to design and lay out for the shop the drawing of a chair that will be satisfactory. No drawing is more deceptive than the full size for a chair, and it is by experience only that a draughtsman can judge what will result from the working drawing. Most draughtsmen of considerable experience, when working out a detail, endeavor to have before them a chair somewhat similar to the one they are drawing.

A good chair should first of all be comfortable to sit in. If intended for general service it ought not to be too heavy to move about easily, and it should be well proportioned.

In planning the seat determine its height above the floor, its width at the front, its width at the back, and the depth from front to back. These vary as desired, and what will make a satisfactory chair for one person, may be quite unsuited to another; consequently there are all sorts and sizes of chairs. It is, however, desirable to have a starting point from which to reckon, and experience has fixed a chair seat eighteen inches above the floor as proper, no conditions being given. If it is less than this it is considered low, and if more it is high. The purpose for which a chair is to be used also serves as a guide for dimensions. If intended for use at a writing table eighteen inches will be satisfactory; if for a dining chair eighteen and a half, or nineteen inches is not too high. Occasionally as high as twenty inches may be used. When the chair is not to be used at a table seventeen and a half, or seventeen inches high is satisfactory for most purposes.

In making the drawing from which a chair is to be constructed care must be taken to determine whether it is to have castors or not. If it is to have them the leg must be shortened accordingly, for the average castor is one and five eighths inches high from the floor to the top of the plate screwed to the under side of the chair leg.

The depth of the seat, that is, the distance from the front to the back, is varied with the height. It is not entirely a matter of appearance, though within limits it may be made to please the eye. Generally, the lower the seat, the deeper it should be. If the chair seat is high, and too deep, the feet of the occupant will not rest on the floor, if he sits back in the chair. Such a chair is uncomfortable, and any one using it either sits on the front edge, perhaps tilting the chair forward on the front legs, or uses a foot stool. Either there is no support for the back or none for the feet when such a chair is used.

A chair that is too low, and shallow in the seat, obliges the occupant to stretch his legs out in front or he becomes cramped against the back of the chair so that almost unconsciously he tips it backwards. Many have tried to devise a rule by which the correct proportion between height and depth of seat can be determined, but thus far none seems to suit all conditions. Approximately, the sum of the depth of the seat plus its height is equal to thirty-five inches.

Chairs for use at a table may be from fifteen to eighteen inches deep; comfortable, upholstered chairs, twenty inches deep; large, low, upholstered chairs may be twenty-four inches deep inside measurement. The width of the seat, from side to side, may be any size called for by the character of the design, except in the case of an arm chair, when it must not be too narrow.

Arm chairs are necessarily wider than others, in order that there may be room between the arms for a person to sit easily without feeling crowded. The space between the arms should not be less than twenty inches at the front edge of the seat, nor less than eighteen at the back. The arm ought also to be of such a height, slope, and length that it will form a convenient rest for the hand and forearm, as well as a side support for the body. Here again arises the conditions of the use of the chair; for, if it is to be used at a table the arm ought not to project forward in a way to prevent placing the chair as close to the table as is desirable for comfort. For such chairs the arm post, that is the upright from the seat supporting the arm, if a continuation of the front leg, is curved backward sufficiently to keep the scroll of the arm back of, or on a line with, the front edge of the chair seat.

The arm post may, however, not be a part of the front post, but entirely independent. Then, it also recedes that the scrool of the arm may be kept well away from the front of the chair. Plate VIII. This arrangement has the advantage of leaving the front of the seat free from obstructions that too closely confine the sitter.

Arm posts on the front edge of the seat interfere with ladies' dresses, and in many of the French chairs the arm posts not only recede, but curve outward at the same time, thus giving considerable more freedom for the person and the clothing.

It is customary to make the width of the seat at the back a trifle less than at the front, in order to avoid the optical illusion of its appearing wider at the back than at the front, as is sometimes the case when the sides are parallel. This difference in width is about two or three inches.

Hepplewhite gives as the general dimensions of a chair: width in front 20 inches, depth of seat 17 inches, height of seat *frame* 17 inches (his chair seats are about 1-2 or 1 inch above the frame); total height 3 feet 1 inch. The height of a chair back is a matter of design, and it may be proportioned accordingly. It may, or may not, be inclined to the seat; its side posts may be slightly inclined, while the middle slopes considerably, thus providing a hollow in which the shoulders of the sitter rest comfortably. Modern chairs usually have the back inclined, though chairs for use in the entrance hall and dining-room are, perhaps, made with the back vertical.

The amount of slope given the back depends on the use to which the chair is put. An easy chair reclines the most, and just as a low chair is deeper in the seat than a high chair, so, too, may the back slope more on a low seat chair than on a high one. A chair with arms may also have a back more inclined than one without.

The appearance of stability is largely influenced by the inclination of the back. So much so, that it is found desirable in most chairs to slope the back legs outwards a little to counteract the apparent tendency of the chair to upset. An arbitrary rule is: the slope of the back for a chair without arms should not be more than one-fourth the depth of the seat and chairs with arms not more than one half.

The legs and rails of chairs should appear firm enough to support, not alone the chair, but the person that sits in it. For chairs with straight legs, whether turned or square in section, the matter of strength is one of size only. The bandy-leg, however, requires more care that the curve may not be too great. Rococo work defies the laws of wood structure, yet it may be properly made so as, in a measure, to reconcile the critic to its eccentricity. In describing the rococo table leg (page 14) it was told how to overcome the apparent, as well as actual, weakness of this form of support, and what was said then will apply as well to chair legs.

Many chairs are more or less upholstered. It may be the seat only that is thus treated, or the entire woodwork, except perhaps the legs, may be hidden by a covering of upholsterer's work.

The simplest methods of upholstering seats are the two padded varieties in which no springs are used. No. 1, Plate XI., shows a cheap way when a hard seat is not objectionable, and it is desirable that there should be a little elasticity. In the illustration the padding is fastened directly to the frame of the seat so when complete it appears the same as an upholstered, spring seat. In some instances the padding is fastened to a separate, loose frame resting in a rebate of the seat frame, and if the chair is turned bottom up the seat will fall out. Such is the way Chippendale and Hepplewhite chairs are often made.

The foundation for the padded seat is webbing stretched as tightly as possible across the frame, front to back, and side to side. The widths interlace, over and under, each other so as to make a firm plaited mat covering the frame. On top of this a piece of burlap is stretched and tacked all round the edge of the frame. On the burlap is spread sufficient curled hair to make the requisite padding of the seat, and this is held in place by a piece of muslin, or cotton flannel, drawn tightly over it and tacked to the side of the frame. The webbing and burlaps are tacked to the *upper edge*. The seat is now ready for any cover that may be chosen, and when at hand the upholsterer spreads it over the muslin cover and tacks it to the frame. The tack heads are afterwards covered by a gimp, which is usually glued on, even though nails are afterwards driven in to apparently secure it. The seat just described is the simplest, as well as the cheapest form of upholstery permissible in good work. It has the disadvantage of being hard, and in a short time the webbing becomes stretched so the seat sags in the middle.

A better seat, requiring a little more work, is shown in No. 2, Plate XI. It differs from No. 1 only in the amount of hair and the way it is used. As there is more hair than in the first instance, the seat frame is made lower that the extra quality of hair may not raise the seat too high.

The hair is placed on the webbing foundation and covered with burlaps. The edges are then stitched by passing a needle in at the side, out at the top, and then back again to the side, and so forth, until the entire edge of the seat has been sewed in this way. When the edge becomes quite hard and firm with the amount of hair that

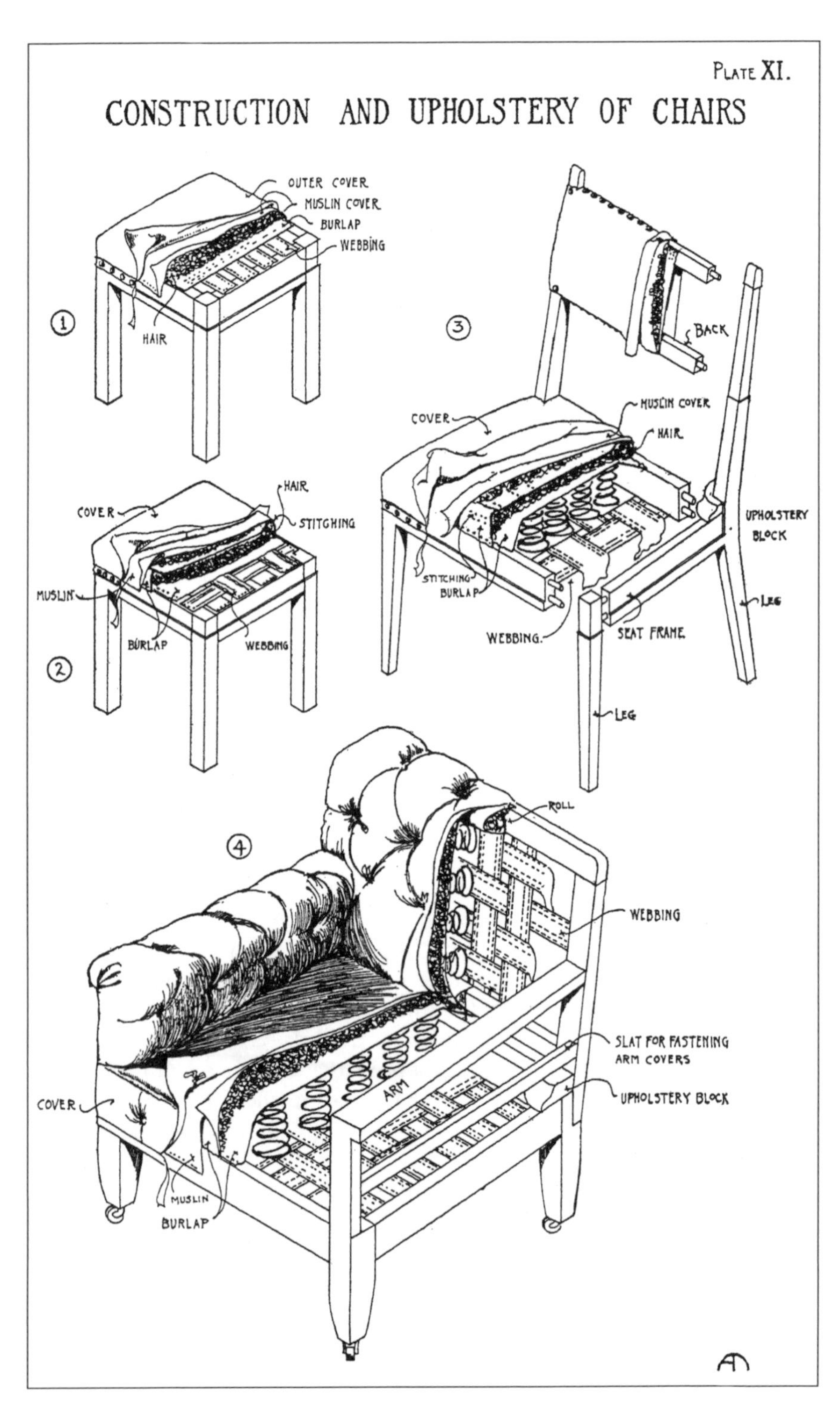
PLATE XI.
CONSTRUCTION AND UPHOLSTERY OF CHAIRS
OUTER COVER
MUSLIN COVER
BURLAP
WEBBING
HAIR
①
COVER
HAIR
STITCHING
MUSLIN
BURLAP
WEBBING
②
③
BACK
COVER
MUSLIN COVER
HAIR
UPHOLSTERY BLOCK
STITCHING
BURLAP
LEG
WEBBING.
SEAT FRAME
LEG
④
ROLL
WEBBING
SLAT FOR FASTENING ARM COVERS
UPHOLSTERY BLOCK
ARM
COVER
MUSLIN
BURLAP

has been stitched in it the middle of the seat is also sewed through and through until it is a trifle lower than the edges. This makes a firm, somewhat hard, hair cushion with its edge a little higher than the rest. The hollow is then well filled with hair, and over this the muslin, and finally the cover is drawn. Such a seat has all the appearance of one upholstered with springs, and is comfortable enough where something firm is wanted.

No. 3 illustrates the spring seat. It differs from No. 2 in this respect: the webbing is fastened to the underside of the seat frame, instead of the top, and on it are placed the springs. Over them is stitched a burlap on which the hair or stuffing is placed. The remainder of the work is the same as for padded seat No. 2. The edge is stitched, hair is added, the muslin is drawn over, and finally the cover.

If it is desirable to make the seat so that none of the woodwork shall show, no difference occurs until the cover is put on, when instead of fastening it, as illustrated, just above the lower edge of the frame, it is brought down over the frame and tacked to the under side. In such work cotton wadding is placed between the frame and the cover that the wood may not be felt, if the hand is in contact with the lower part of the seat.

Chair seats that are upholstered have a block of wood notched around the corner post on the inner side, and fastened to the top of the seat frame, where it joins the back. This is the "upholstery block," and is needed by the upholsterer to tack the cover on where it fits around the back post. The upper surface of this block is about one-half inch below the level of the finished seat.

Chair backs may be upholstered in a manner similar to seats, and the methods are the same. The term "over-stuffed pieces" is applied to furniture that is upholstered so that none of the framework, except the legs, is visible. No 4, Plate XI., illustrates an arm chair of this description, showing the framework and the method of covering it. The frame is of hardwood, and is constructed the same as any other chair. The seat frame is set low in order that there may be plenty of room for large springs, making the seat soft and easy.

Beneath the upper rail of the arm, and also of the back is a second rail left loose that it may be fastened where desired by the upholsterer. These rails are used by him for fastening the lower edges of the arm and back covers, which are put on after the seat is upholstered.

The seat frame of overstuffed pieces should be so constructed that the webbing may be tacked to it at a point not more than eleven inches below the level of the top of the springs, if springs of usual dimensions are used. It may be less, if desired, for then smaller springs can be used, or large springs may be tied down. The top of the seat is about two and a half inches above the top of the springs. Sometimes the seat frame is very deep, and were the webbing tacked to its lower edge the springs would be much below the level required. In such instances either a strip of wood is fastened all round the inside of the frame to which the webbing may be tacked or else an extra loose frame is covered by webbing and set inside the seat frame at the proper level.

The upper edge of the seat frame is usually about halfway between the level of the webbing and top of the springs. The method of upholstering the seat and back when springs are used, is the same as described above for No. 3. In the work on the back, however, there will be noticed on the illustration a portion marked "roll." This is made of hair stitched in burlap to make a firm edge, all round the back frame, possessing elasticity enough not to feel hard when leaned against. Over this the covers are drawn.

In good work the upholsterer carefully covers all edges of the wood with hair stitched in burlap and all flat surfaces with cotton batting, so that at no point is the wood beneath easily detected by the touch.

Overstuffed pieces do not admit of a great variety of good forms. There are no end of patterns, or designs, in which an attempt has been made to produce something new and good; but most of them are unsatisfactory.

The beauty of this class of work is dependent on the absence of fussy, unnecessary trimmings, and on the outline. This outline ought to be one that seems the natural result of using upholsterers' materials, and the simplest best fills this requirement. Upholstery may be either plain or tufted, and the choice is at times a matter of taste, but frequently tufting is a constructive necessity. When the seat level is high above the frame tufting of the front edge prevents, to a degree, the sagging of the covering when the chair is occupied and the springs compressed. A border formed by a line of stitching along the front about half the height of the seat sometimes serves the same purpose. These methods also prevent the cover from appearing too large after the piece has been used awhile and the stuffing is matted down. It is also advisable to tuft the seat and back of very large pieces for the same reason; or, as a decorative feature if the covering material is plain, unfigured goods. The tufting should always be proportioned to the size of the article. Where the surface to be upholstered is concave tufting is necessary, otherwise the material can not readily be made to follow the curve. The ordinary form of tufting is to sew the goods in at the four corners of a diamond, but occasionally for concave surfaces it becomes more like a series of rolls side by side and the full length of the hollow.

The material used as a cover for over stuffed pieces largely affects their appearance; goods that would be well suited to one chair may not look right on another. The color is governed by the decorations of the room in which the furniture is placed. It need not, perhaps should not, be the same color as the walls since contrast is desirable, but it must be in harmony with the surroundings. The pattern of the goods may be of a historic style similar to the design of the room, though it does not seem necessary to confine oneself too closely, for in many instances the figure of the goods is entirely lost in the tufting, and a color effect is all that impresses itself on the mind. This is largely true also of pieces without tufting.

It is well to avoid patterns too pronounced in form or out of scale with the article covered. Then, too, it is not desirable to use designs composed of objects that a person would not care to sit on, as shells, sharp tesellated forms, musical instruments, buildings, landscapes, etc. The suitable materials are those woven with an "all over" ornament of a size adapted to the intended use, and treated in a flat way without imitating modelling in relief.

Over stuffed articles have no woodwork, except the legs, showing and they sometimes seem too light for the mass above, though really they may be more than strong enough. If fringe is hung from the lower edge of the upholstery to the floor the feet are hidden and the general mass is apparently resting on the floor, the fringe serving to carry the color and lines to that level. The length of the fringe may be about one-half the height of the seat. The best taste admits of only simple fringes free from small drapings, "skirts," or elaborate nettings that soon become dirty and shabby. When the supports of the furniture are sufficiently heavy to suggest no thought of weakness, and there is a frame to show wood below the upholstery no fringe is required.

The rush seat chair is not in common use, as it was a number of years ago, yet occasionally it is wanted. The frame for such a seat is shallow, not more than an inch and a quarter, and has all its edges rounded. Sometimes the frame is nothing more than turned sticks over which the rushes are twisted and woven into a seat entirely covering them.

The cane seat requires a flat frame usually above the seat frame, though it may replace it. On the inner edge of this frame holes are bored through which the cane is drawn and stretched across the opening until a seat is formed.

The sofa is practically an extremely wide chair, and the data given for chairs may be applied to it.

The following is a table of dimensions of various chairs taken from satisfactory examples:

CHAIR DIMENSIONS.

Variety.	Height.	Seat. —Width.— Front.	Back.	Depth Out-side.	—Back.— Height.	Slope.	Arms. Height. from floor.
Bedroom chair	18	16	13	17	34	2½	..
Baby's high chair[1]	20	14	12	13½	37	3	27
Cheek chair[2]	17	29	25	27½	44	4½	..
"Chip" chair	17	22	17½	17	39	..	..
" "	18	22	17	17¾	38	..	..
Dining chair	20	24	22	22	45	2½	26½
" "	20	19	17	19	43	2	..
" "	19	19	17	18	38½	1½	..
" "	18	20	15	15	36	2	..
Easy chair	17	33	28	*24	43	5	21
Easy chair[2]	17	27	25	27½	41	6½	26
"Hepplewhite" chair	18	21½	17	17	34½	2	27
Parlor chair[3]	16½	24	19½	18¾	36	4	25¾
Parlor chair[2]	14	21	21	*18	29	..	..
Parlor chair[2]	18	26½	22½	26½	37	4	25
Parlor chair[4]	18	20	13	19	36	3	23
Piano bench	20	40	..	15	..	..	..
Reception chair[5]	17	21	19	21	30	2	..
Rocking chair	16	23½	20½	19½	41	2	24
"Roundabout" chair	18	18	18	18	29½	0	28½
"Rubens" chair	20½	17½	17½	15	40	0	..
"Slipper" chair	12	18	15	17	28	3	..

[1]Foot rest 12 ins. above floor; [2]overstuffed; [3]French cane seat and back; [4]wood arm and back; [5]upholstered seat.
*Depth inside.

SOFA DIMENSIONS.

Variety.	Height.	Seat. —Width.— Front.	Back.	Depth Out-side.	—Back.— Height.	Slope.	Arms. Height. from. floor.
Small	18	43	40	21	32½	3	24
Extra large	16	78	76	36	29	2	25
Ordinary sofa	15	54	51	24	34	5½	24
Lounge	17	68	68	28	35	2½	29
"	17	57	57	29	23	12	34

Note.—All dimensions are given in inches. Heights are above the floor. Slope of back is measured, at seat level, to a perpendicular through highest point of the back.

CHAPTER IV.

Casework, Panelling, Bedsteads.

THE beauty of casework is dependent on: Firstly, its proportion as a whole. That is whether the height, the width, and the depth are of dimensions that appear well together. In most problems at least one of these dimensions is fixed by some requirement of utility. The designer is then expected to decide the other two.

Secondly, the disposition of the parts (i. e. panels, framing, architectural members, such as columns, mouldings, etc.), of which the case is composed has its influence on the design. Whether the panels are large, or small; whether they are arranged in pairs, or grouped in another way; whether the mouldings are heavy or light, etc., are the questions studied.

Thirdly, the ornamentation. This is the last point to be considered, because if the general form is bad no amount of decoration, whatever its quality, will make a good piece of furniture. As the subject of the ornamentation of furniture is treated as a separate chapter (VI.) it need not be discussed further here.

In front elevation casework usually approaches more or less the form of a rectangle and the first condition in its design is to find a method for determining the ratio of the sides of a rectangle most agreeable to the eye. This has already been studied by several writers with at least two solutions.

One assumes a square as the starting point and implies that any rectangle having two sides equal to the sides of the square will be well proportioned if the other two sides are not more than twice its length. In other words, a well-formed rectangle is not more than two squares long. Plate XII.

Another ratio given is that of two to three. Assuming that if the width of the rectangle is two, the length should be three. This ratio, of course, is included within the limits of the first method.

For the purposes of designing it may be assumed that the rectangle, whether vertical or horizontal, represents the principal mass of the case. What is technically known as the body. To this may be added at the top the crowning members, and at the bottom the base on which the whole is supported. To the sides may be added the projections of mouldings, columns, brackets, or other decorative features.

The relation of the various parts to each other and to the whole should be kept in mind. Often casework consists of an upper and lower section. The lower part must not only be sufficiently strong to support what is above it, but it ought to appear so without seeming heavier than is necessary. The base or feet should be proportioned to the mass above and the crown members, well supported, are to be made large enough to serve as a finish for the case without apparently crushing it.

The spacing and arranging of the principal lines dividing the case into panels, drawers, etc., is to be such as will give pleasing results, and there are an infinite number of arrangements possible. The whole mass may be divided into two equal parts by a post the same size as one on each corner of the cabinet, No. 3, Plate XII. This sort of a division has the disadvantage of causing the case to appear as if it were made of two smaller ones placed together, and as if the two parts were balanced on the middle line. It is not considered the best way of doing.

A similar composition is one in which the case is divided into three parts with the middle one the smallest. This has the faults of the former method, though not in such a marked degree. When three divisions are made the best appearance is obtained by making the middle one larger than those each side of it. No. 6, Plate XII. Other arrangements are also shown on the same plate.

As was mentioned above, furniture should be adapted to its use, and if possible its design should indicate the use. The location of an article in a room has its effect on the appearance. So much so, that if possible the designer should study the surroundings. He is then in a position to make a design that will harmonize with the decoration of the room, and an article of a size best suited to the space it will occupy. He can also see how much light will fall on it and be governed somewhat by this in determining the size of the mouldings, etc. If the room is well lighted a moulded member if fine and delicate will show to advantage, but in a dark corner larger moulding will be more suitable.

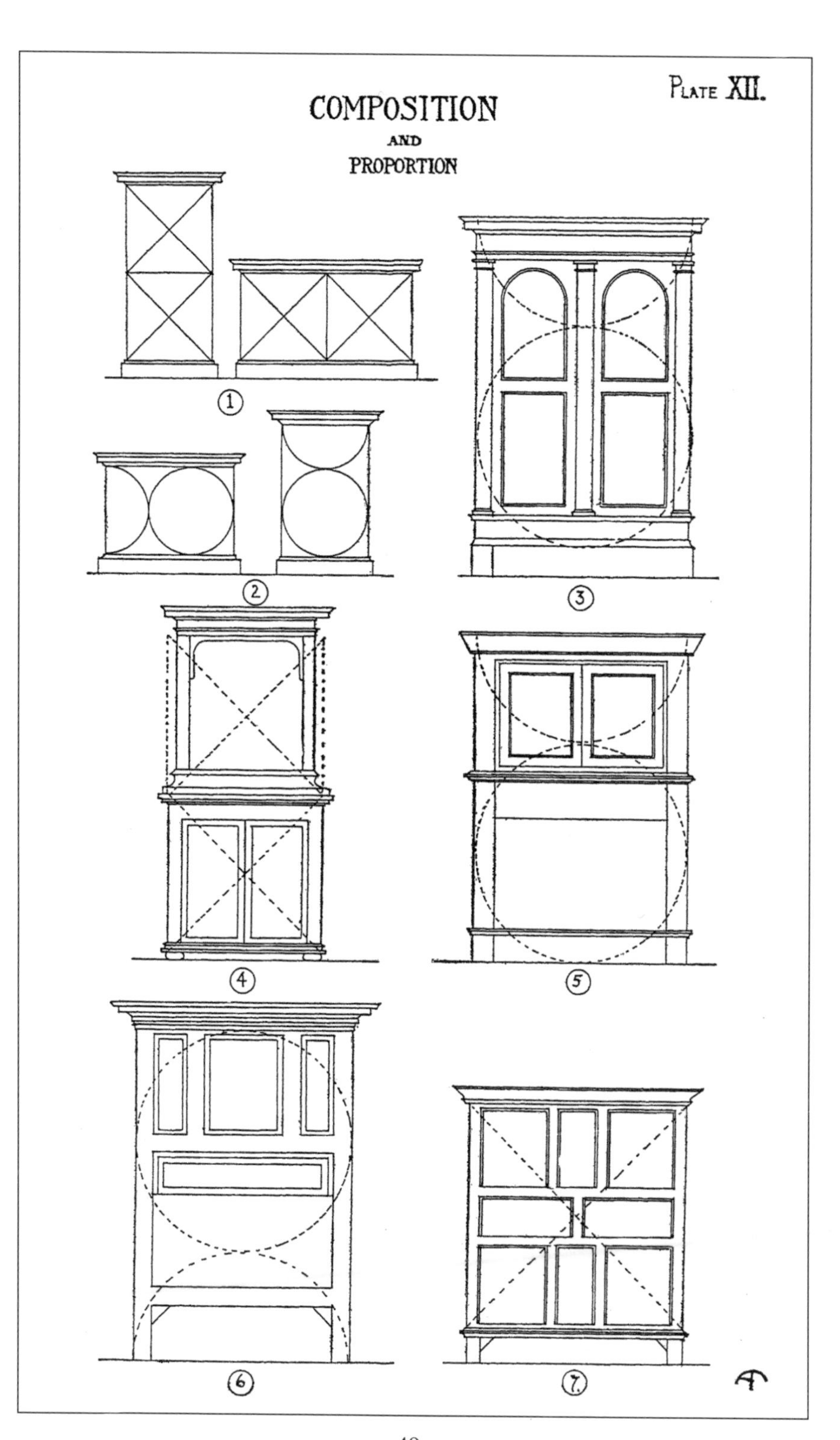
PLATE XII.
COMPOSITION
AND
PROPORTION
1
2
3
4
5
6
7

As casework pieces are usually the largest in the room they are quite prominent, no matter how simple they may be, and care must be taken not to make their presence obtrusive by over ornamentation. The decoration used should be appropriate, sparingly applied, and of the highest quality of execution. Casework approaches nearer to architectural designing than any other furniture draughting. In nearly every article mouldings are used that are identical with those of architecture. They are combined in the same way and their use is for much the same purpose. There are eight forms from which nearly all others are derived by combination or variation and their names are of importance as serving a means for description.

Plate XIV. illustrates these mouldings as follows:

The *fillet* is a narrow, flat surface, usually above or below another moulding, and it may be either a projecting or receding member. When below the surrounding surface it is a *sunk fillet.*

The *bead* is a small, half-round moulding either projecting from or even with the surrounding surface. In the latter case there is a narrow grove at one side, and it is called a *quirked bead.*

The *cavetto* is a hollow moulding, the outline of which does not exceed a quarter circle; and the *ovolo* is the reverse of the cavetto; that is, a projecting member of which the outline is a segment not exceeding a quarter. The cavetto and ovolo are not always circular in outline. Any curve may be employed, but the circular or elliptical form are most common.

The *cyma recta,* or *ogee,* has a profile composed of two arcs hollow and convex, like a wave, the hollow at the top. The crown member of cornices is often made with this moulding.

The *cyma reversa,* as its name indicates, is the reverse of the ogee; the convex curve is at the top and the concave below.

The *scotia* is a concave moulding with the outline a segment of a circle often greater than a semi-circle. It is sometimes called a thumb moulding, and the hollow section is then composed of two tangent arcs of different radii.

A *torus* is a large convex moulding usually with a semi-circular profile. When any of these mouldings are used beneath a horizontal surface forming an angle with a vertical one it is called a *bed mould.*

Later we will see that mouldings used to hold panels in place are sometimes partly above the surrounding rails. They are then called *raised mouldings* to distinguish them from *flush mouldings* which are level with the rail. Mouldings serve various practical purposes but their æsthetic effect is to be thought of. They produce much the same result, when used as a frame, that a line border does about a drawing. The effect of light and shade on a moulding is to produce a series of lines that vary indefinitely, according to the proportions of the moulding and its parts. A deep undercut moulding gives a heavy dark shadow, a black line; and a narrow flat moulding a light shadow; a fine line.

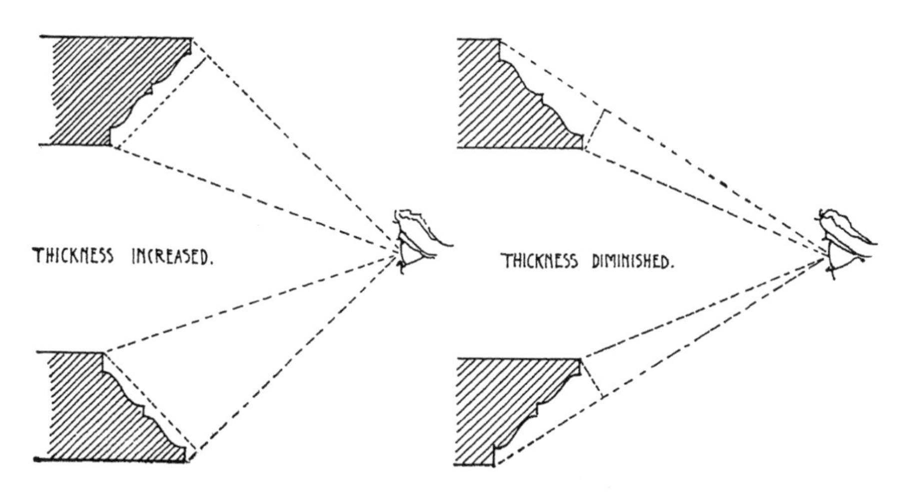

EFFECT OF MOULDINGS.

The position of the moulding in relation to the eye may also apparently increase or diminish its members. If it is placed above or below the eye so the moulding ascends or descends, respectively, and recede from the eye the member will diminish in size, appearing thinner than it is. On the other hand, if the moulding descends or ascends respectively the member will appear thicker than it really is.

When a moulded member is composed of two or more of the simple forms described above it owes its charm somewhat to the introduction of a fillet which separates each moulding from that adjoining. An important combination of mouldings is their use in the crown members of cabinets. We have already called attention to having this proportioned to the size of the body below; in addition, it should not project too much. If its overhang is not greater than its depth it will usually look well, but in many instances it will be found desirable to keep somewhat within this limit.

Mouldings may be ornamented by carving and when so treated

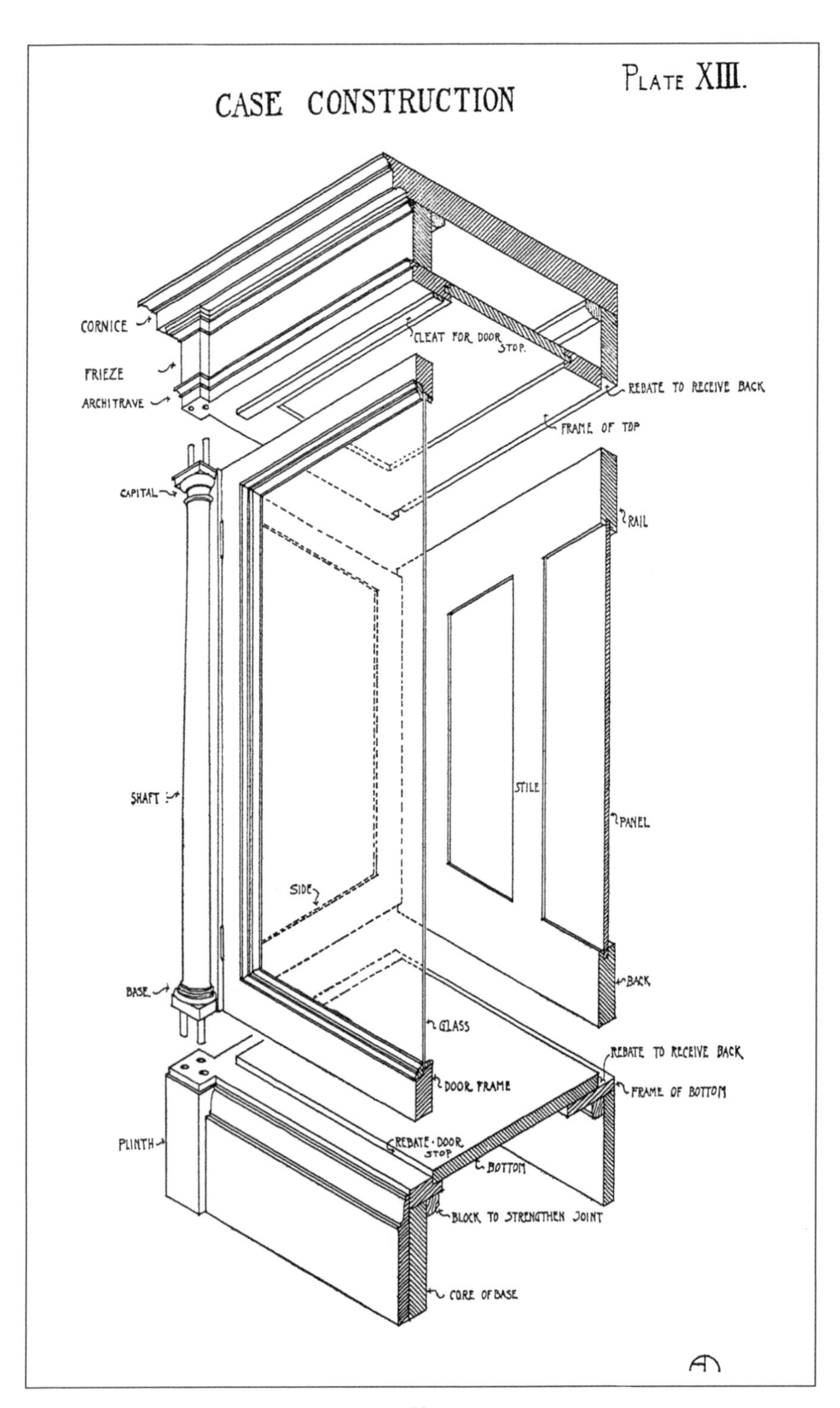
CASE CONSTRUCTION
PLATE XIII.
CORNICE
FRIEZE
ARCHITRAVE
CLEAT FOR DOOR STOP.
REBATE TO RECEIVE BACK
FRAME OF TOP
CAPITAL
RAIL
STILE
SHAFT
PANEL
SIDE
BACK
BASE
GLASS
REBATE TO RECEIVE BACK
DOOR FRAME
FRAME OF BOTTOM
PLINTH
REBATE·DOOR STOP
BOTTOM
BLOCK TO STRENGTHEN JOINT
CORE OF BASE

care must be taken to preserve their general form. It is usual on architectural members to employ the profile of the moulding as the leading line of the ornaments upon it. Thus, the fillet may be decorated by vertical lines as flutes, fret, or dentils; the bead, by "pearls," bead and spindle; the torus by the guilloche; the ovolo, by an egg and dart; and the cymas, by the heart ornament, etc.

Cases are composed of a top, a bottom, and uprights between which are panels of wood or glass. Plate XIII. shows a section of a cabinet with the parts separated so as to illustrate how it is constructed. The column forming the corner post is doweled to the base and cornice. The sides and back are paneled and are either doweled or rebated to the other parts. The bottom and top is composed of a frame

JOINTS

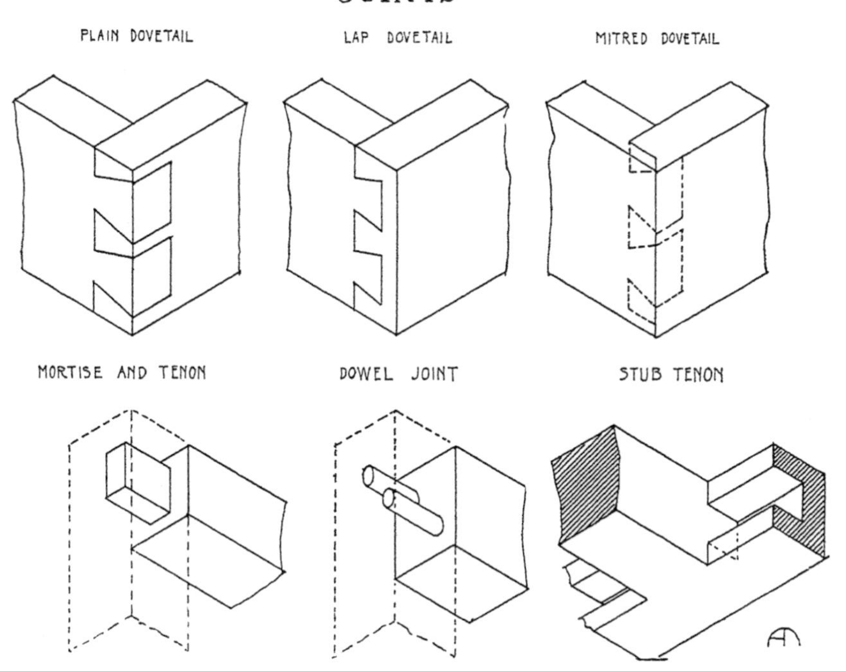

surrounding a panel. In order to build all parts together use is made of several kinds of joints. Though these are not always shown on the drawings it is desirable that the draughtsman be familiar with them. They may be arranged in three groups, comprising those commonly used in furniture construction; the butt, the angle, and the framing joint.

The butt-joint is employed when two pieces of wood are jointed together in the same plane. The simplest form is when the edges of the two pieces are brought together and held by glue, no other connecting medium being used. This is often sufficient, and when properly made is quite strong. It is almost invisible in the majority of woods when made so the grain is parallel with the line of contact.

When a stronger method is required, and one side of the pieces joined is hidden from view, blocks are glued across the joint, on the unexposed surface, so as to stiffen it. The grain of these blocks must be parallel with that of the jointed pieces that shrinkage may not loosen, or cause them to crack.

Another way of uniting the edges of two boards is by the tongue and groove. A tongue, or projecting piece, along the middle of the edge of one piece is matched to a groove in the edge of the other. Sometimes in place of this, a groove is cut in the edge of each of the boards throughout their entire length. Into these grooves is then glued a hardwood strip, called the tongue or slip-feather, uniting the two pieces.

The most popular joint with the cabinetmaker is the dowel-joint. It is perhaps the best where the wood is of sufficient thickness to permit its use. A dowel is a wooden pin used for fastening two pieces of wood together by inserting part of its length into one piece, the rest entering a corresponding hole in the other. Sometimes a number of dowels are fitted tightly into holes bored for them in one of the pieces to be joined, and the other has corresponding holes bored in it, in which the dowels also fit tightly when the two pieces are glued together.

Angle joints are frequently mitred; that is, the joined edges are cut at a bevel bisecting the angle between them when united. The union is made by butting the pieces and gluing them together. As this does not make a strong joint in itself, it is stiffened in various ways. One method is to drive small bits of corrugated metal in the ends of the pieces and across the joint, thus binding the parts together. At other times corner blocks are glued on the inner side of the mitred angle.

For rounded corners, or when a mitred angle is not wanted, the two pieces may be tongued and grooved together. The tongue is on the inner edge of one of the pieces, so that as much wood as possible is retained outside the groove on the other. The best and strongest method of joining two pieces at an angle is by dovetailing.

When the joint is made so the full thickness of each piece joined is visible and the shape of each dovetail can be seen the joint is a *plain dovetail*. The lapped dovetail is constructed so the joint is seen at the side only, and is commonly used for fastening the sides and front of drawers together. When it is desirable to have all indications of the dovetailing hidden, a combination of the mitre and dovetail is used, in which the dovetails are cut in part of the thickness of the wood and the mitre in the remainder. Such a joint is a mitred dovetail.

The usual framing joints used by furniture makers are the dowel-joint and the mortise and tenon. (See also page 17.)

The true mortise (cavity) is cut near the end of one piece to receive the tongue (tenon) of the other. The tenon is not always the full width of the piece on which it is cut, but often is narrower.

When framing for a series of panels, a groove is sunk the whole length of two of the framing pieces (those extending horizontally, called rails), and those at right angles to them (vertical pieces between the panels, the stiles) have tenons cut on them which fit in the grooves. These grooves also receive the panels. This method avoids cutting a mortise for each tenon, and the name given to the joint is *stub-tenon.*

When two pieces are joined by cutting away half the thickness of each and then lapping them together, they are said to be *halved.* Such a joint is sometimes combined with a mitre, so that where exposed to view it appears like any mitred joint. It is then said to be *halved-mitred.*

Broad surfaces of casework are panelled partially as a means of decoration, but principally for constructive reasons. If the surface were made from a solid board, it would soon crack and warp as the wood became dryer. It might be built up and veneered as has been described for table tops (page 18), and this is occasionally done; but as paneling gives a change of plane with a chance for light and shade, it is more commonly used.

The panels are, however, veneered and cross-veneered on both sides of a core whenever perfect workmanship is wanted.

Panels are surrounded by a frame, which may be grooved to receive them; but a better way is to rebate the frame and hold the panels in by mouldings. Three ways of doing this are shown on Plate XIV. In the joiner's method either a groove is worked in the styles of the surrounding frame to hold the panel and then the moulding is placed in the angle against the panel, or a rebate is cut in which both panel and moulding are set.

In either case, if the moulding is nailed in, the nail will probably be driven directly in the panel, or else diagonally through both the edge of the panel and rail. In the first instance any shrinkage of the panel causes a crack to appear between the frame and the moulding.

To avoid this, a rebate can be cut in the moulding, when it is large enough to permit, so it will lap over on the frame a little and hide the joint.

But here, although (see illustration) the nail holds the moulding close against the frame, it also catches the edge of the panel and prevents it moving. The result is that cracks appear in the panel itself.

It does not improve matters much if the moulding is glued in, for the glue almost always binds both moulding and panel to the frame, so that a rupture will occur somewhere.

The cabinetmaker avoids these difficulties. First he cuts a rebate in the frame on the finish side. In this the moulding is *glued* solidly so it becomes a part of the frame itself. When the glue is dry the *varnished* panel is set in from the back and held in place by plain mouldings nailed to the frame. This leaves the panel loose and free to move should shrinkage take place. The object in varnishing the panel before setting it is that if any movement does occur it will not be seen by the exposure of a line of unfinished wood.

Flush panels are so named because their surface is level with the surrounding frame. They are set in a rebate from the back and secured by a nailed moulding. In most cases a bead is run all around the edge of the panel, so as to hide the joint between it and the frame. Such panels are used for the back of cases and in places where no decorative effect is wanted.

Panels may have the edges beveled or rebated below their surface, so as to produce a sort of border around the panel itself. Such panels are sometimes spoken of as raised panels, to distinguish them from a flat, even surface.

The surface of a panel is made of more carefully selected wood than that used for mouldings and rails, with the intention of having a handsome grain. Veneers are chosen that have been cut from a portion of a log furnishing strong markings, or "figures," when polished, and these are sometimes cut in smaller pieces, either half or quarter the size of the panel, and placed together so the lines of the grain will form a pattern, or a "picture." At other times a design is inlaid on the panel or it is carved. The simplest form of carved

MOULDINGS AND PANELS

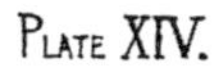

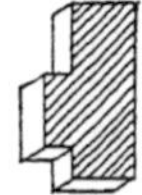
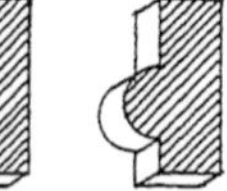
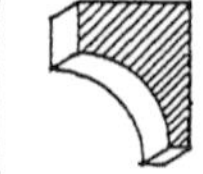
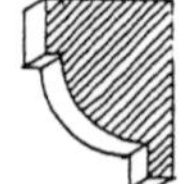
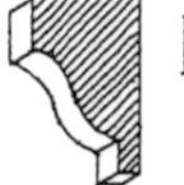

FILLET. BEAD. CAVETTO. OVOLO. CYMA RECTA AND REVERSA. SCOTIA. TORUS.
OGEE.

CLASSIC MOULDINGS

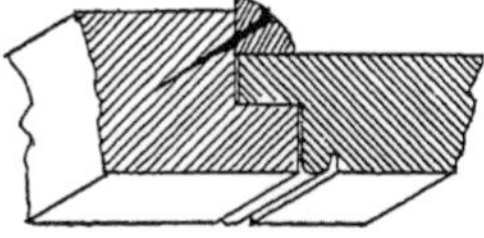
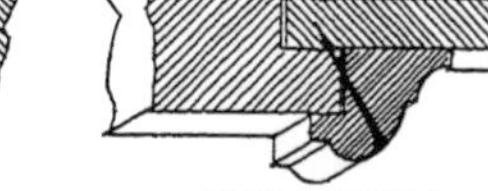
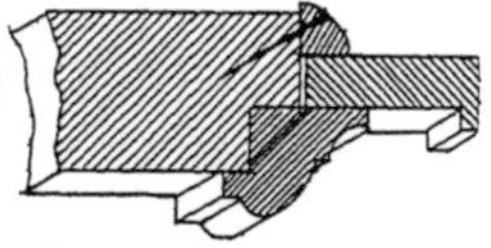

FLUSH PANEL. JOINERS METHOD. CABINET MAKERS METHOD.

METHODS OF SETTING PANELS

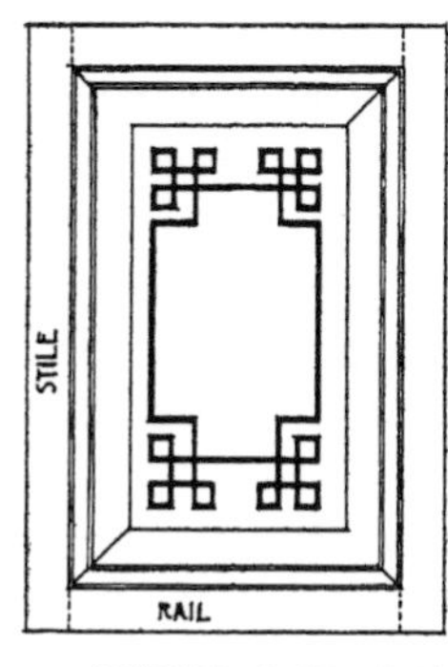

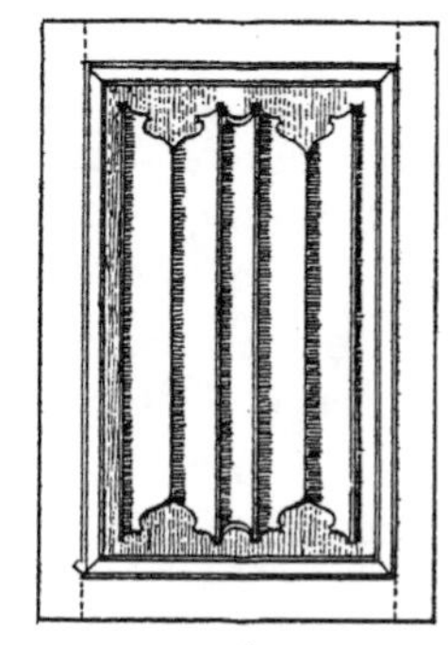

BEVELLED PANEL INLAYED. "PARCHMENT" PANEL. CARVED PANEL.

TREATMENT OF THE PANEL SURFACE

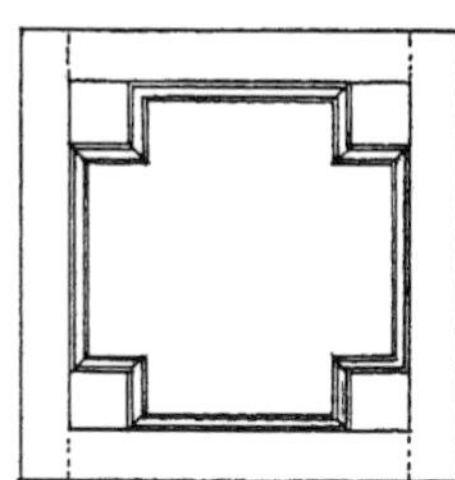
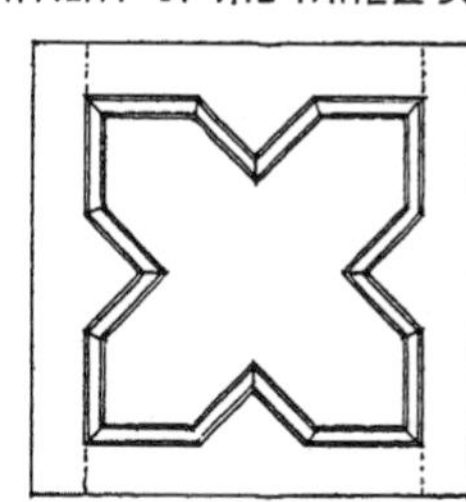
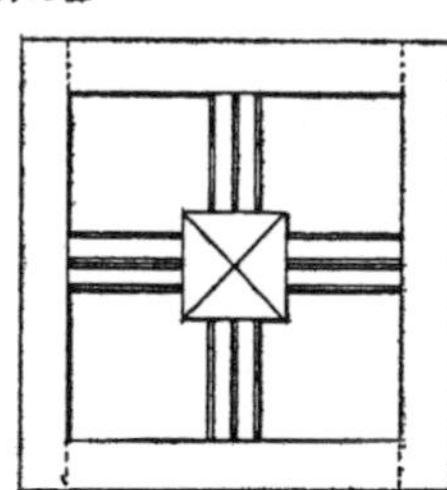

FORM OF PANELS

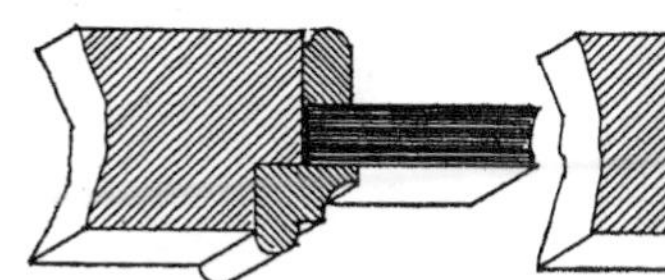

GLASS FULL SIZE AS A PANEL. GLASS ON BLOCKS. MIRRORS. BEVELLED GLASS.

FRAMING GLASS

panel is that with the surface moulded to resemble, more or less, the folds of drapery, and called linen or parchment panels.

By arranging the mouldings around flat panels, so as to produce forms with a broken outline, the stiff rectangular panel is avoided. Three varieties are shown on Plate XIV.

Bookcases, china cabinets and others of the same class of casework have portions of their sides glazed either with clear glass or mirrors.

In the best of glazed work plate-glass is used, but where something less expensive is wanted the best quality of double-thick sheet glass is used. Anything poorer than this should not be placed in good work. Mirrors should always be of plate-glass. Glass set in doors or substituted for panel work is cut the full size of the rebate opening in the frame, and is held in place by a loose moulding, the same as a panel. Plate XIV. It is only when some special condition requires it that the glass is secured in place by putty and glaziers' points instead of the loose moulding.

Mirrors are not often cut to the full size, but are a trifle smaller than the rebate measure, and the glass is held in place by a number of triangular blocks, about three inches long, placed at intervals in the rebate. These blocks serve to wedge the glass securely in place, that it may not slide in the rebate, and they also reduce to a minimum the surface of wood in contact with the coating on the back of the mirror.

The silvering is protected from injury by a paneled backboard, screwed to the frame after the glass is fastened in. This backboard must not touch the mirror at any point.

The glass is held in front by a moulding set in a rebate, as we have described for paneling.

Doors are composed of a framework enclosing panels. The uprights of the frame are the *stiles,* and the horizontal parts are the *rails.* They are hung either with hinges or pivots. The former are more or less visible, but the latter are concealed. Plate XV. illustrates various applications of these methods. No 1 shows the door hung with butts and without a rebate for the door to shut against. Such a door would be used in cabinets where the uninterrupted joint between the edge of the door and the side of the case is not objectionable. Notice also that unless the door can swing through an arc of 180 degrees the width of the opening is reduced by about the thickness of the door, or A in the illustration. In most instances a rebate to receive the door is desirable; and still the door hung with butts would reduce the size of the opening, as at A, No. 2, unless the rebate is as deep as the door is thick, No. 3.

Doors for cabinets having drawers within are hung this latter way, as it enables one to pull out the drawer, though the door is open at the right angle only. No. 4 shows how a door may be hung when the design calls for a pilaster on the corner of the case and yet the conditions require that a maximum width be given to the interior. An article having the door hung in this manner must stand sufficiently away from the wall or other pieces of furniture to permit the pilaster to turn on the axis of the hinge.

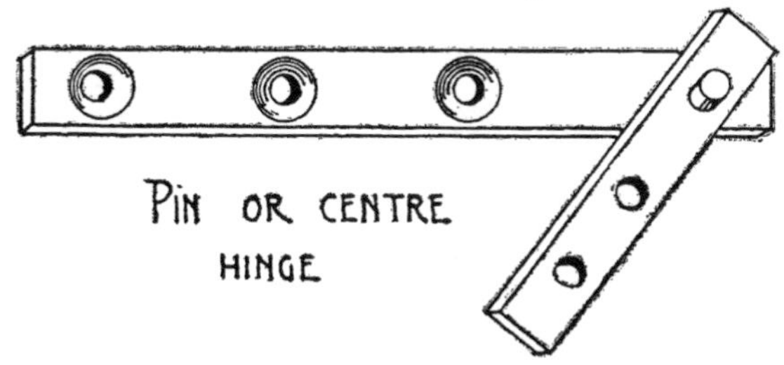

The pivot, pin, or center hinge, is invisible, and in high-class work this is an advantage. It is also strong, and is screwed to the upper edge of the top rail and the lower edge of the bottom rail of the door in a position such that a strain does not start the screws. The illustrations shows what it is like. There are two bars of metal, narrow enough to be entirely concealed by the thickness of the door. In one of these bars is a hole receiving a pin on the other bar. One of the bars, that with the socket, is set in the frame receiving the door; the other is on the door itself, and when complete the door turns on the pin as an axis.

It is well to set the pivot on a line through the middle of the thickness of the door and about half the thickness of the door, plus an eighth of an inch, away from the post against which the door turns; that is, $C = B + 1/8$ inch. No. 5 shows a pivoted door in a position where it reduces the width of the door opening, and No. 6 shows the pivoted edge of the door turning in a hollow prepared for it and provided with stops, against which the edge of the door strikes either when open or shut.

The thickness of door rails is dependent entirely on the size and design of the door, but the bottom rail is made a little wider than the top rail and side stiles, which are of the same width.

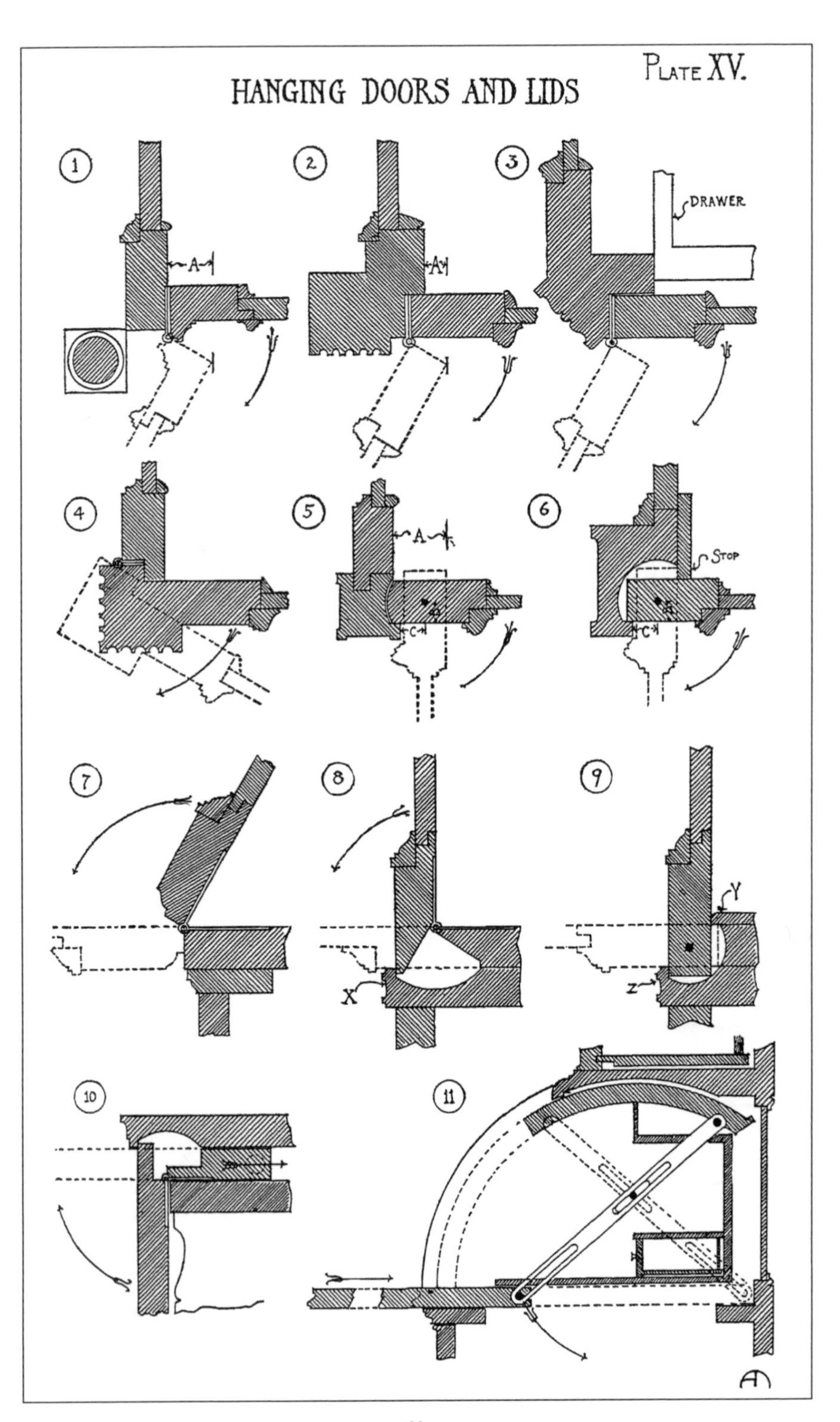
PLATE XV.
HANGING DOORS AND LIDS
1
2
3
DRAWER
A
A
4
5
6
A
STOP
C
C
7
8
9
Y
X
Z
10
11

The meeting stiles of a pair of doors are sometimes rebated, so the joint does not extend straight through.

Sliding doors may be provided with rollers at the bottom or the top, or they may slide in a groove without aids for reducing friction. Sliding doors are often in pairs, and then it is necessary to arrange that they close tightly at the meeting stiles, which overlap a little.

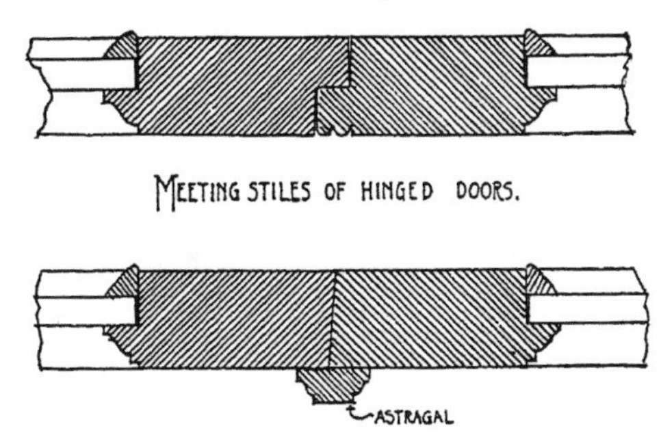

MEETING STILES OF HINGED DOORS.

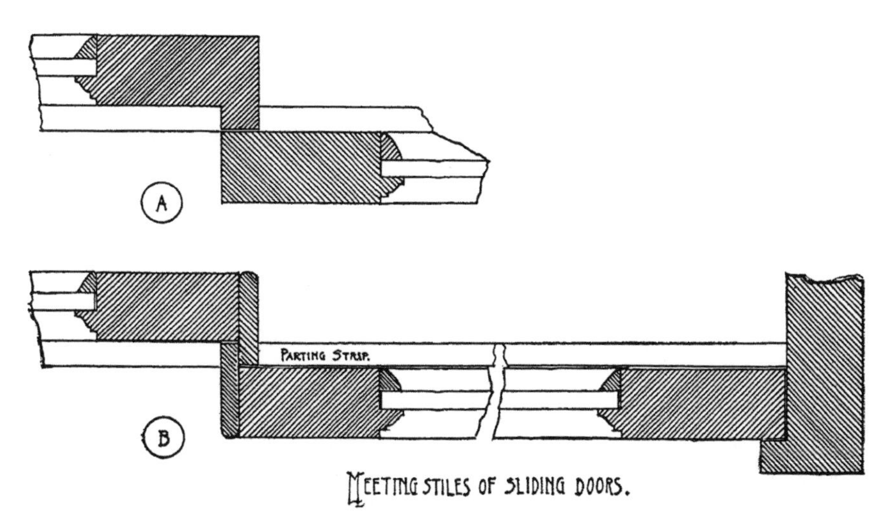

MEETING STILES OF SLIDING DOORS.

There is more or less space between the doors, due to the thickness of a "parting strip" at the bottom and top, forming the groove in which the door slides. To close this space a thin strip, sufficiently wide to extend across it, is fastened to the back edge of each door. When the doors are closed these two strips are in contact and lap over each other.

Desk lids may be considered as doors hung by the bottom rail, but they seldom open wider than an angle approximately 90 degrees, and the method of hinging is dependent on the way the lid is supported.

When ordinary butts are used, it is necessary to have slides that pull out beneath the lid for it to rest on, or else metal elbow pieces, chains or quadrants are fastened above. Otherwise the weight of a person's arms on the lid when it is down will break the hinges.

Illustration No. 7, Plate XV., represents a section of a lid hung in this way, and No. 8 is a method without slides or quadrants that may be used for lids of cabinets where no great weight is to come on them and butts are used. Here the hinge is not directly on the edge of the lid, but is set a little beyond it, the lid and hanging stile having been cut on a bevel to permit the lid swinging down to the horizontal. A portion of the case (X), just below the lid, is also arranged so the lid when down will rest on it.

The strongest lid hinge is the pivot. No 9, Plate XV. The lid when down presses against Y and Z, and the hinge itself is constructed so as to take part of the strain.

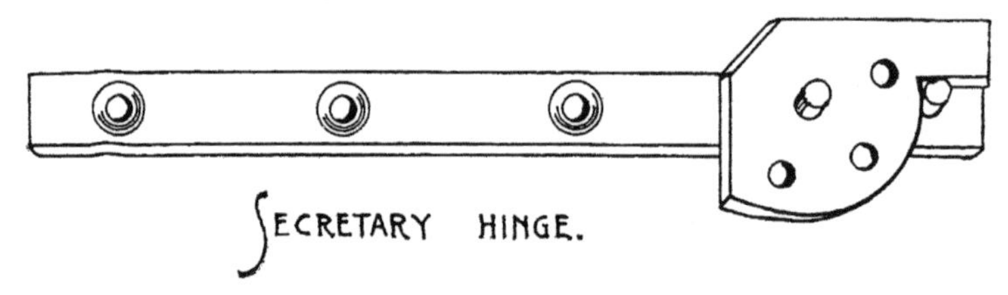
SECRETARY HINGE.

It is practically the same as the pin hinge described above. The part serving as a socket for the pin is, however, shaped somewhat like a rectangle, with a small projecting square on one side near one corner. The other corner of the side from which this square projects is rounded off as a quadrant, with the socket for a center. The pin bar is also extended sufficiently to receive a second pin, located so that it just clears the edge of the quadrant when the two parts of the hinge are placed together, and will strike against the projecting piece of the socket plate.

If now the socket plate is properly fastened to the side of the cabinet, the parts of the hinge are in the position shown in the illustration when the lid is turned down. The second pin of the bar strikes against the projection on the socket plate and acts as a stop. This brings the greater strain on the metal of the hinge itself. The location of the pivot on the edge of the stiles is such that the screws are not pulled out if an extra strain is put on them. As in every drop lid, there is more or less leverage; there will be some spring when weight is applied to it. It is therefore advisable to use aids for support—either quadrants or braces.

The lid for small compartments of desks, or the desk lid itself, may be hung so as to raise and then slide back out of the way. A section of a lid of this kind is given in No. 10, Plate XV. The dotted line shows the position of the lid raised and ready to be pushed back into the pocket. When the lid is down, the upper edge strikes against the back of a moulding, so as to hide entirely the pocket into which it slides when raised. The hinge is on the lower edge of a rebate cut in the lid. This rebate matches a similar one cut in a strip fitted so as to slide easily in the pocket, yet provided with stops to prevent its being pulled out. When the lid is raised, this guide and the lid halve together, so as to become practically one piece.

The cylinder top desk is made so the lid will slide back into a pocket, the edges of the lid moving in grooves cut in the sides of the desk. When the desk is small, a lid working in this way does not slide back sufficiently to expose a convenient writing surface. The difficulty is overcome by making the writing surface so it may be pulled out about two-thirds the depth of the desk, and the pigeonholes, with the inkstand, etc., may be placed immediately above at the back of the desk. This arrangement makes quite a roomy writing table of one that would otherwise be small. It is convenient to construct such desks so one operation will pull out the slide and open the lid, instead of requiring each movement to take place separately.

There are many ways of doing this, and the one illustrated (No. 11, Plate XV.) is by Sheraton. A metal bar is pivoted to the edge of the lid near the back and it is similarly attached to the slide. This bar has a slot cut at the lower end, in which the pivot on the slide may move, and another slot near the middle, in which moves a pivoted guide attached to the side of the desk. This latter pivot is the central paint about which turns the bar connecting the slide and lid; so when either is moved the other moves also. There are two of these connecting bars, one at each end of the desk.

Shelving in cabinets and bookcases are made so as to be adjustable to any heights. Sometimes they are supported by four pins, one at each corner of the shelf, placed in holes bored in the sides of the case. These holes are one inch or more apart, and by changing the location of the pins the shelf is adjusted.

At other times four vertical notched strips are fastened to the ends of the case, two at each side, and in the notches cleats are placed on which the shelves rest. By shifting the cleats the shelves are placed as desired.

The following is a table of dimensions taken from existing examples of case work:

DIMENSIONS OF CASEWORK.

Variety.	Body.			Remarks.
	Width.	Depth.	Height.	
Bureau	45	20½	36½	
"	51	23	37½	
"	48	22	36½	
"	54	20	42	
Bookkeepers' desk	60	33	42	
" "	60	32	44	Deck 11 ins., slope 22.
Chiffonier	39	20	48	
"	36	20	51	
Cheval glass	25	..	65	
Commode	16	16	31	
Sideboard	84	32	30	
Wardrobe	36	19	69	
"	54	24	96	

Note: All dimensions are in inches.

Bedsteads.

Bedsteads have a head board, a foot board and two side rails. The head and foot board are often panelled, and sometimes the side rails also. In the old-style bedstead there were four posts. These were joined together in pairs by a rail above, which was a second rail more or less elaborately decorated by sawing, carving, turning or panelling, thus making the head and foot boards according to the position they occupied when united by two rails that formed the sides of the bedsteads.

The side rails, with the lower ones of the head and foot board, formed the frame, across which cords were stretched to support the mattress. In the modern bedsteads the arrangement is much the same, except that in many of them the post is reduced to its lowest terms, and exists only as the stile for the panel work of which the head and foot board is composed.

The side rails are made much wider than in olden times, that they may hide the box spring, which has taken the place of the cording, and they are constructed so they may be removed and replaced as desired. There are many contrivances for accomplishing this, each manufacturer having his preference.

A strong and substantial way is shown in the illustration.

The ends of the rails are provided with tenons that fit mortises in the posts of head and foot boards, and with screws that work in nuts sunk in the posts. These screws fasten the rails and end boards securely together, while the tenons stiffen the joint, preventing any twisting of the sides.

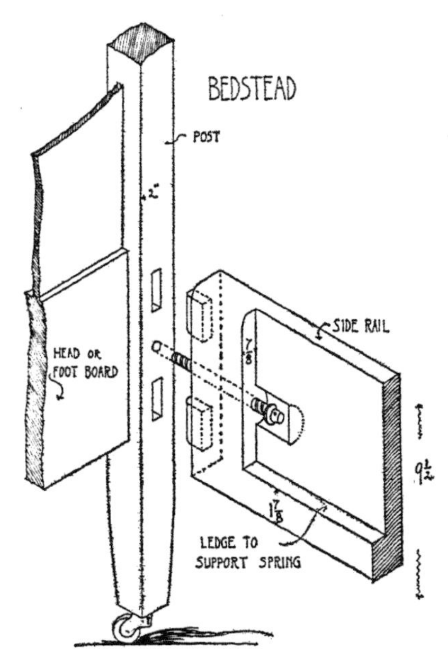

On the lower edge of the side rails, inside, is a ledge to support the spring. The box spring is sometimes supported on slats and sometimes on the side rail of the bedstead, a cleat having been placed on it so as to rest on the ledge of the rails.

The mattress is placed on the springs. In designing a bedstead it ought to be constructed so the top of the mattress will not be much over twenty-five inches above the floor.

Bed slats are about an inch thick, a double box spring about ten inches thick, and a good mattress seven inches thick.

To keep within the limit of height, then, the upper edge of the support for the slats should not be more than seven inches from the floor. But slats are sometimes omitted, and then the side rails may be set higher, so the springs can hang a little below them without being seen.

The following is a table of measurements of bedsteads:

DIMENSIONS OF BEDSTEADS.

Variety	Inside. Length.	Inside. Width.	Height. Foot.	Height. Head.	Width. Side Rail.	Height. Bottom Side Rail
Single	78	42	40	62	9½	9½
"	78	42	41	60	10	10
Double bed	78	58½	42	63	11	10½
" "	78	56	36	67	13	9½

Note: All dimensions are in inches.

CHAPTER V.

The Drawer. Plate XVI.

NEARLY every article of furniture may be provided with a drawer; and the ease with which it slides and its accuracy of fitting are tests of good workmanship. To have a wide, deep drawer slide so easily that the pressure of a finger placed against the front at one end is sufficient to move it, means careful adjustment, skilled labor and the best materials.

The drawer is composed of a front, back, two sides and a bottom. The front is the only part visible when the drawer is closed, and upon its treatment depends the decorative value of the drawer. It may be considered as a panel surrounded by mouldings, or it may be left plain, depending on the hardware for its ornamentation.

If the front is on the same plane as the surrounding surfaces of the case, the line of the joint about the drawer is too clearly defined. It is better to hide this joint by allowing the drawer to slide in a sixteenth of an inch beyond the face of the framework, or to place a bead all around the edge of the drawer.

Sometimes the front of the drawer has its edge rebated, so that, instead of sliding into the pocket beyond the surface of the case, it projects beyond, and the lip of the rebate covers the joint around the drawer. The sides of the drawer are dovetailed to the front, and the bottom is either grooved directly in the sides or in strips glued to them. This latter method is used when the sides are too thin for grooving. The full thickness of the bottom is not grooved into the front and sides, but its edge is reduced in thickness by beveling or rebating, thus permitting the bottom to be placed low without making the portion of the sides below the groove too thin.

The space between the lower edge of the drawer front and the bottom at its thickest part is about one-eighth inch. Hence the interior depth of a drawer is the depth of the front minus the thickness of the bottom plus one-eighth inch. The average drawer, having a bottom of half an inch, would therefore have an interior depth five-eighths of an inch less than it appears on the front. Wide drawers, like those extending the full depth of a bureau, sometimes have the bottom divided through the middle from front to back by a rail or muntin. This prevents the bottom from bending beneath the weight placed on it, and also decreases the tendency to warp. The bottom should be long enough to extend beyond the back piece. It is also grooved into the front where it is fastened, but it ought not to be secured elsewhere. This method of construction admits of the bottom shrinking, but as it is fastened on the front only and free to move elsewhere, it will not crack; and the extra length beyond the back prevents an opening appearing at that end.

The back may be grooved or dovetailed in the sides. The dimensions of the different parts are dependent on the size of the drawer. For ordinary work the front is seldom more than seven-eighths inch thick, and the sides, bottom and back more than one-half inch.

In casework the drawer slides in a pocket, and often there are several drawers, one above the other. When enclosed, the drawer slides on a supporting frame, the front rail of which is called the "bearer," and the side rails "runners." Close against the sides and supported by the runners are narrow strips of wood, that serve to keep the drawer in place. These are the "guides."

Sometimes the frame between the drawers is open, and if one of the series is removed that beneath may be emptied by reaching through the opening above. In better work the frame is fitted with a panel, called a dust panel, that prevents this.

The drawer is not always enclosed. Sometimes it is hung beneath a table top and exposed to view. When used in this way, cleats are fastened to the outer surface of the sides and slide in grooved pieces screwed to the underside of the table top. If the cleats set close to the upper edge of the sides of the drawer, they increase the thickness of this edge, which is in contact with the under surface of the table top. As this surface may not be true, the drawer will not work smoothly unless hung loosely.

A better arrangement is the one illustrated, with the cleat set a little below the edge of the drawer and fitted smoothly in the grooved bearer. The edge of the drawer may then be set so as not to rub against the top of the table, and yet the drawer is held secure by the cleats sliding in the grooved supports. Sometimes the groove is in the side of the drawer and the bearer is provided with a tongue that fits it, reversing the method just described.

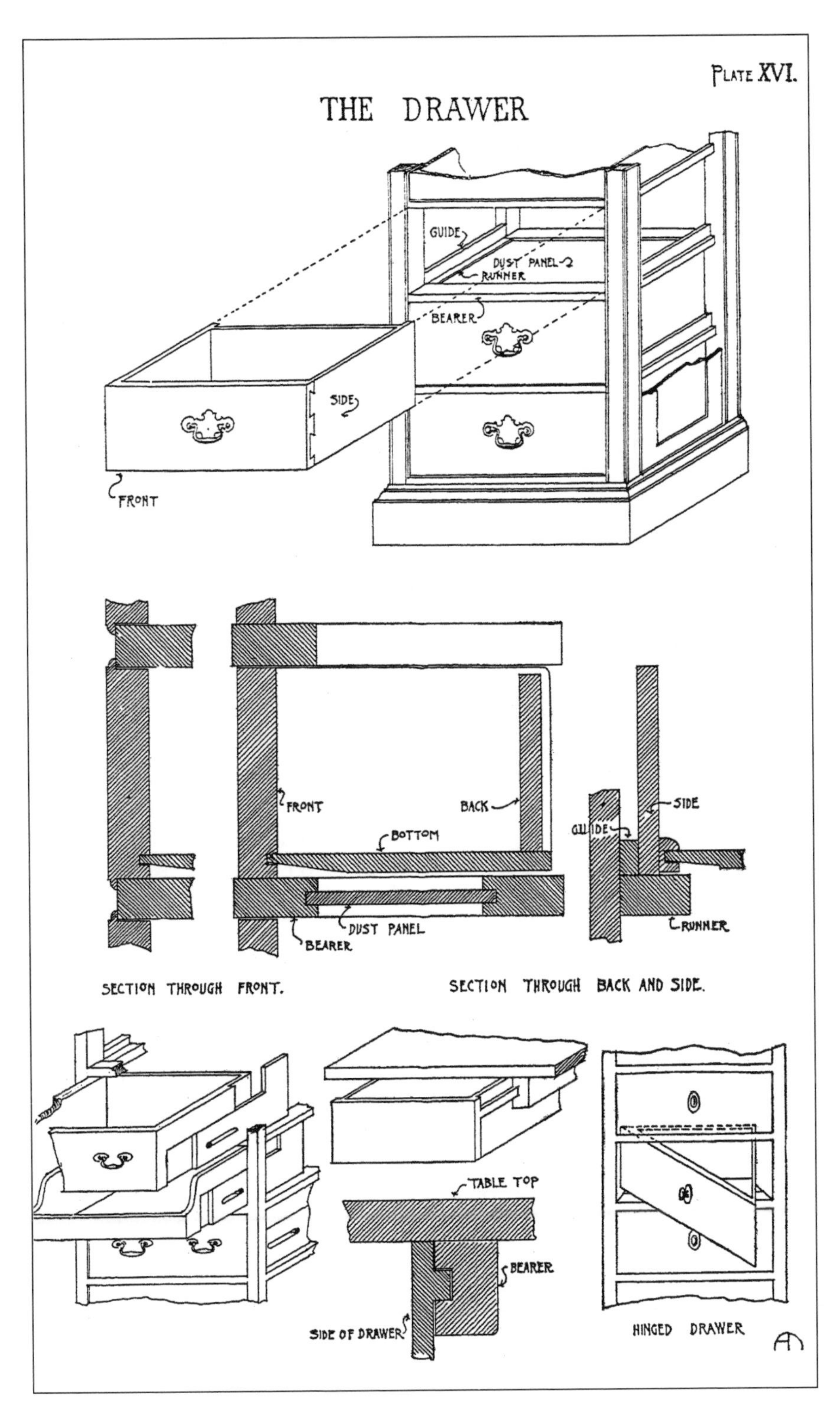
PLATE XVI.
THE DRAWER
GUIDE
DUST PANEL
RUNNER
BEARER
SIDE
FRONT
FRONT
BACK
BOTTOM
DUST PANEL
BEARER
SIDE
GUIDE
RUNNER
SECTION THROUGH FRONT.
SECTION THROUGH BACK AND SIDE.
TABLE TOP
BEARER
SIDE OF DRAWER
HINGED DRAWER

When it is desirable to place a drawer in a piece of furniture having a triangular plan, as, for instance, a corner cabinet, the guides at the side are useless, as the drawer does not come in contact with them except when pushed in. As soon as the drawer is pulled out ever so little it no longer fills the width of the pocket. If it is necessary to slide a drawer of this shape, a rail is placed in the middle of the bottom the length of the drawer from front to back. The underside of this rail is grooved over a tongued strip immediately beneath it, that serves as a guide to keep the drawer in the middle of the pocket. Such an arrangement is not always feasible, and then the triangular drawer is pivoted at the front edge; so instead of sliding it swings out of the pocket.

For music cabinets, library cases, etc., the use of the drawer may make it necessary to pull it out sufficiently that the entire length can be seen. A drawer constructed in the usual way would, if pulled out so far, fall to the floor as soon as the hand left it. A drawer is made, however, with slides at the sides that support it when out its full length. The illustration shows such a method. The side of the drawer is about twice as thick as ordinarily, and the lower portion is rebated about half its depth and thickness. In this rebate a slide it fitted, exactly filling it. The rear end of the slide is increased in width to the full depth of the drawer. When the drawer is closed the slide and the side of the drawer are practically one. When the drawer is pulled out to a fixed point the slide catches against a stop and does not move any further, but the drawer then moves along the slide until it is nearly or entirely out of the pocket, when it is stopped by a pin moving in a groove in the side of the slide. The drawer is then resting entirely on the slides, which are sufficiently far in the pocket to carry the weight, and the widened portion at the rear end of them filling the space between the runners prevents upsetting.

When a pair of doors close against a case of drawers another system may be used in place of the above. The doors can be hung so as to open to a position in the plane of the sides of the cabinet and held there by stops. Their inner surface may also be provided with runners, on which the drawer can slide when it is pulled out beyond the pocket.

CHAPTER VI.

Ornamentation of Furniture.

IN addition to the general outline and proportion of furniture, its appearance is dependent upon ornamentation. This should not, however, become so important as to destroy the constructive elements or the utility. A properly designed article may be quite as pleasing when entirely devoid of ornament as when its surfaces are covered by enrichments of some sort.

In many instances what is termed ornament is but a roughening of coloring of the surface, in hopes to divert the attention from bad forms or poor construction. It is understood that woodwork free from surface ornament must be well made, the wood carefully selected, and care taken to use together pieces of the same color and figure of grain. The joints, unless properly made, become conspicuous, exposing the poor workmanship. The finish—that is, the varnishing and rubbing, must be well done, that the wood may not appear to be covered by a candied surface full of lumps and streaks. Work well made and finished feels to the hand almost as soft and smooth as silk velvet, while to the eye the grain of the wood shows clear and sparkling beneath the thin, well rubbed film of varnish which fills the pores yet scarcely more than covers the surface. In such work the beauty is dependent upon pleasing outlines, good proportions and workmanship. The smallest details, like softening the angle, rounding a corner, etc., require attention, because of their influence on the appearance of the whole.

There are times when it is desirable to do more than fill the demands of service, and additional expense may be incurred by enriching the simple form with decoration.

There are several methods of doing this. Perhaps the most difficult to do well, and yet the most common, is carving. It can be used as a surface ornament, treated as a panel, either cut below the surface of the wood, or in relief. The constructive parts, as posts, rails, mouldings, etc., may be also in ornamental forms. In the first instance—panel work—the problem is one of designing an ornament to properly fill the space, keeping in mind the effect of light and shade. The pattern is in relief of varying planes, and the different parts must be of a size that will be in keeping with the space filled as well as the entire article.

The ornament may closely fill the whole space or be loosely scattered over the surface, but in either instance it should seem to belong where it is, and not as if it might be placed elsewhere or was floating about in a space much too large for it.

In some kinds of furniture may be seen small ornaments in high relief cut from a block glued in the middle of a plain surface many times the length and width of the ornament. Such carving appears as if stuck on, even if it is well executed; for it is wrongly placed and inadequate to the space it occupies. It is not because it is glued on that makes it uninteresting, as might be supposed, but because it is badly designed. Had the surface of the solid wood been cut away to leave carving of the same design in relief, a similar feeling of its having been applied would exist. Nevertheless, the practice of gluing on carving should be discouraged.

When the constructive parts are carved, care should be taken to design the ornament so the contour of the part is not destroyed. Instead of detracting from the form, it ought to enforce it. This may be accomplished by keeping the principal masses of the ornament well within the boundary lines of the part decorated and by making the ornamental growths follow the direction of the structural lines.

If the carving is on the surface of a chair back where it may be leaned against, it should not be of such a high relief as to be disagreeable or so sharp as to be dangerous to the clothing. The illustration given (frontispiece) here is an example of over-ornamentation and exquisite carving misplaced. It is a chair with the arm post finely and skilfully carved, but so delicate in its detail as to be almost too frail for practical use. And so rough and sharp are the angles that should a delicate dress be pulled across it it would probably be torn.

Plain surfaces have quite as much value as those that are ornamented, and by bringing them in conjunction, so as to secure a contrast, the best results are obtained.

It has been mentioned in a previous chapter (page 10) that the wood used for the construction has an influence on the design. This is especially true of carved ornament. Although it may be possible to do delicate carving in the coarse grained woods, it is certainly not good taste to do so. In the close grained woods, like satinwood, mahogany and maple, we expect to see delicate and fine work, while in oak, ash and walnut we at once look for a different sort of thing.

Carved surfaces, with the background cut entirely through—that is, perforated—are serviceable forms of ornamentation for chairs, tables, and occasionally for case work.

What has been said relative to surface carving is applicable to this style of work. The design ought to be of a kind in which the spaces and the solids balance each other properly, and no portion should be cut around so as to leave it joined to the rest of the work at one point only. Aside from the poor appearance of such a form, it is weak in construction and likely to split off.

Plate XVII. illustrates perforated carving in use on chair backs, and shows how the parts are joined. It will be noticed that the perforated ornament is confined to the slat in the middle of the back, one-half of which is drawn as it appears when finished, while the other half is only blocked out ready for ornament.

This is quite clear in the shield-back design, where the middle slat is simple in form. The other chair has a more elaborate slat, and its character as such is almost hidden by the form of the ornament. It should be noticed in designing a back of this sort that the general outlines are first determined, keeping in mind the constructive principles. In the chair illustrated the outline of the back is drawn first; next the ellipses composing the slat, and finally the carving. This latter follows carefully the lines of the composition, so as not to destroy the original forms. The acanthus on the sides of the center ellipse lap close about it, and as the opening in the middle of this ellipse was too large for practical purposes or appearance the group of husk ornaments was placed in the middle.

Where the top of the slat, in the form of a horizontal ellipse, joins the top rail of the back a dowel is placed. The thickness of the material included in the outlines of the ellipse is hardly sufficient to make a strong joint, and to have increased the thickness at this point only would have destroyed the appearance of the design, unless some way had been taken to prevent it.

This was done by turning a scroll at the point where the dowel occurs and filling in between the scroll and top rail with a small acanthus. This gives the increased material without injuring the appearance, and is a rational method of using carved ornament.

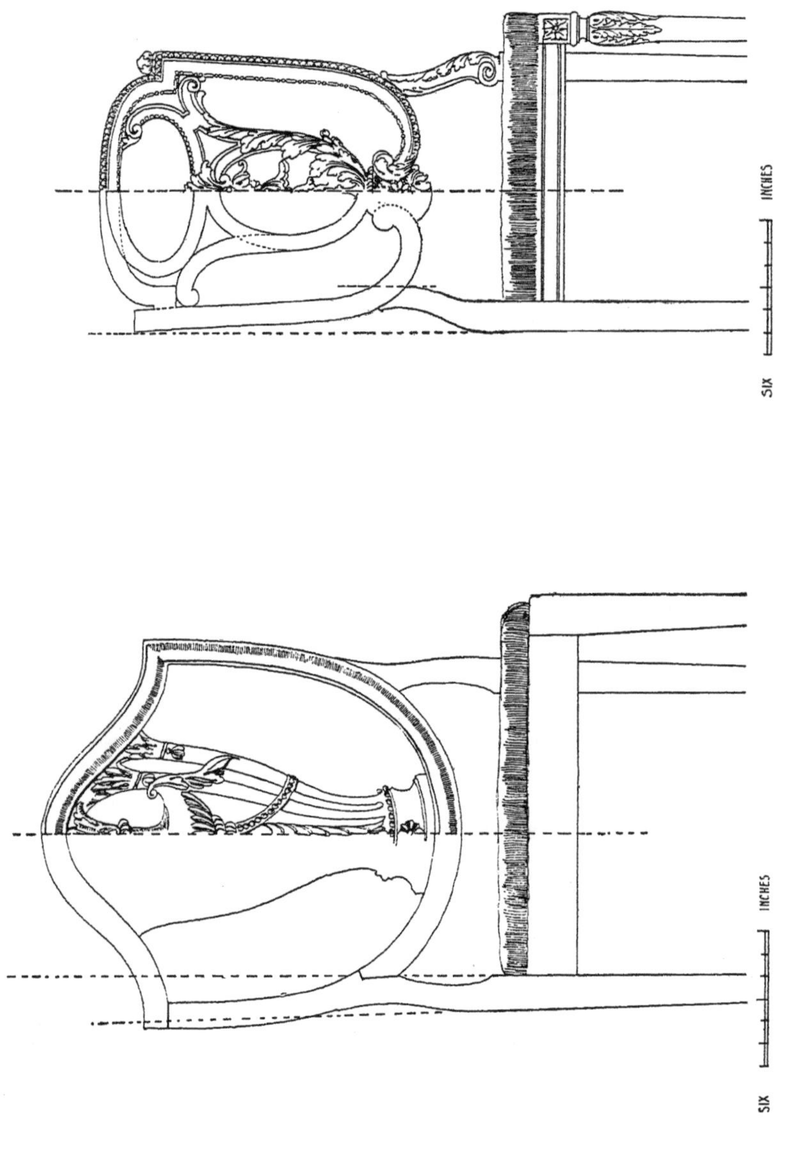

PLATE XVII

SIX INCHES

SIX INCHES

PLATE XVIII.

LOUIS XV. TABLE. METAL ORNAMENT APPLIED WHERE STRUCTURAL CARVING MIGHT BE USED.

PLATE XIX.

LOUIS XVI. CABINET. METAL APPLIQUE AS ORNAMENT ONLY. NOT PLACED ON STRUCTURAL LINES.

Applique of metal work is a form of relief ornamentation, in many respects closely related to carving. It may be either cast or wrought. Castings, called ormolu, are usually of brass plated with gold and finished a dull color. They are especially used in the styles of Louis XV., Louis XVI. and Empire. In the Louis XV. style much of the ornament is applied in places where carving might have been used, and it is properly joined with the lines of the article so as to become a part of them. In the Louis XVI., to some degree, and in the Empire style almost entirely, the applique ornaments are fastened directly on a plain surface without any relation to the construction whatever, as the article is complete without them. The beauty of their use depends on the arrangement of the pieces in relation to each other, the way they fill the space which they occupy, and on the design and execution of the metal work itself. Much of the metal work in ordinary use is poor in both respects. Perhaps the design is good and the pattern was well modelled, but so many copies have been made, each cast from a previous moulding, instead of from the original pattern, that all form and crispness is lost. Such work is neither handsome nor decorative, and the designer should discourage its use whenever he can. In the best French examples, applique metal work is carefully cast, exquisitely chased, so it becomes a beautiful piece of workmanship, and it may be admired as such, even though its use is not approved. When wrought metal work is applied to furniture it is usually in the form of hinge plates, lock plates or ornamented straps binding parts of the woodwork together. Furniture decorated in this way is best made of a coarse grained wood and designed with large, flat surfaces, on which the metal may be applied for ornamental effect. Good results are obtained by sinking the metal work so it is level with the wood surface, particularly when in the form of rosettes.

The markings of the grain of woods used for furniture is in itself an ornamentation, and many times it is quite sufficient. But to increase its decorative effects veneers cut in various ways are used. A veneer is a thin slice of wood, and in the choice woods of the furniture maker many pieces with rich figures in the grain can be had as veneers that otherwise could not be obtained in shape to use. Then, also, by cutting a log in different ways, the beauty of the grain is exposed so that its value is increased.

The veneers are not always used entirely like so many boards. They are sometimes cut in geometrical patterns, varying in size, and the pieces placed side by side in such a manner that the grain of adjoining pieces runs in different directions, thus covering the surface with an almost inconspicuous diaper pattern.

In this method of using veneers but one kind of wood is required, though at times two or more may be used. When a color effect is wanted, marquetry is used, introducing the various colored woods, metal, shell or ivory, in the form of ornament on a ground of the wood of which the furniture is constructed.

There are no special difficulties to be avoided in designing a pattern for inlay. Almost any ornament that appears well in flat colors will make good inlay, so that the problem is one of designing a conventional ornament suited to decorate the space when rendered in flat colors.

The nearest approach to inlay is ornament painted on the surface of the wood. This has been a common and handsome method of decorating furniture, though it is not now popular. One method is to treat all the ornament flat, similar to inlay; another is to paint natural forms in a realistic way. The ornament is sometimes painted on the varnished surface of natural wood, and, again, it is placed on an enamel. In one class of work, painting is executed on a panel first covered by silver or gold leaf, the design introducing figures, pastoral scenes, architectural compositions, etc.

The surrounding parts of the article are thickly varnished, and at times specks of gold leaf are mixed with the varnish. Such work is more or less an imitation of Japanese lacquer work, but is known as Vernis Martin, because during the reign of Louis XV. the brothers Martin secured the exclusive right to make furniture varnished in this way, they claiming to have discovered the secret of making the lacquer used.

There remains another means for ornamenting the plain surface of furniture woodwork. That is by burning on it with a metallic point an appropriate design. It is a method that lends itself to successful treatment in proper hands. Such examples as are most frequently seen are not desirable, largely because the patterns burned are not suitable. The color effect is, however, charming, running from soft brown tones of a pale color to a deep rich black. A combination of carving and burning gives satisfactory results. The wood may be light in color, like white maple, and the carving somewhat of the Indian (Hindoo) order. This, when complete, has the edges and background burned by a cautery. The work then, varnished in the

PLATE XX.

XV. CENTURY CABINET.
WROUGHT METAL APPLIQUE AS ORNAMENT IN THE FORM OF HARDWARE.

usual manner, resembles a little old ivory carving, and is well suited to certain rooms.

Whatever form of ornamentation may be used, it should be borne in mind that no amount of decoration will make a poorly proportioned or badly formed article good. It may be possible to divert the eye for a time from the general shape by placing before it a multitude of small details, but these will generally become tiresome, and the article will then be considered as a whole.

In all design work it is not a question of how much ornament, but how well the ornament may be designed. It is advisable to use it sparingly, erring, if it may be, one the side of too little rather than too much. The object of ornament is to decorate the otherwise plain surfaces. and if it does not do this it is better left off.

The sources of pleasure in all decorative designs are the beauty of forms employed and the sense of study having been given to their composition. There is satisfaction in examining a piece of ornament to find it has been arranged with some regard to the massing of the parts, instead of being merely placed at random in a careless way. The pleasure of discovering the plan on which an interesting ornament was built has been experienced by every designer. The foundation should not be so prominent as to be forced on the mind, but it may be so well conceived that a thoughtful study will disclose it hidden among the beautiful forms of which the composition is made up.

What may be termed visibility demands attention in the disposition of ornament. Much labor and expense are wasted by placing the decorative features in positions where they are not seen, or if seen, it is to a disadvantage. There is no reason for a finely executed ornament so near the floor or far under a table or chair that it cannot be seen without getting on the floor; nor is there any sense in decorating the frame of a table which is presumably to be covered continuously by a cloth.

Though everyone recognizes the impropriety of the bad disposition of ornament in this respect, it is not easily guarded against. The designer will find, unless he is extremely careful, that he has indicated on his drawings work that will be entirely lost to view.

CHAPTER VII.

Theories of Design, Rendering, Etc.

IT is necessary that the designer should be familiar with the historic styles of architecture and furniture. He should also study the characteristic forms and ornamental details of each period. This will enable him to recognize the kind of furniture needed to harmonize with surroundings, learn what has been made, and store his mind with material that suggests new forms and ideas. In many instances the designer is required to make his work correspond with a historic style. Then his best course is to hunt up good existing examples of the style (not necessarily the articles he is working on, but any in the style), and with these before him try to give their character to the problem. When not restricted in any way, he should work out the forms suggested by the purpose for which the furniture is used. Study this purpose and consider the character of the material used in meeting it. By working with a knowledge of these requirements, a design may be made that does not resemble any style. It is more probable, however, a close adherence to the demands of the problem will lead to the employment of a style, and it is well that it should, as then some good example may be taken as a model. There are excellent models for modern furniture in all styles, though many of them may not be suited to exact reproduction, owing to change of customs. But, when possible, furniture should have the characteristics of some recognized style.

Many poor designs are due to a striving to produce something new and original, different from what is seen every day. The result is rarely pleasing. Any article that is designed with the intention of making it odd, peculiar or picturesque is usually poor. Aim to make it beautiful; not by disregarding styles, but by working upon rational methods. The result will be furniture with possibly but little ornament, and it may be noticeably plain and simple. But it is not desirable that all furniture should be richly ornamented, and overloading with ornament is, of course, to be avoided. Study good examples, whether ancient or modern, and if an article appeals to you as particularly good try and find why it does so. Make a memorandum of it and put it in a scrap-book for future use. Often, a long time after seeing several objects, it happens that some one of them is recalled vividly, while the others are forgotten. This impression is caused either by the value of the material from which the object is made, the beauty, the ingenuity of mechanical construction, or the eccentricity of design, and it should be valued accordingly.

The secret of successful study is the knowing what to select and how to use the material on hand. To know what not to do is almost as good as knowing what to do. It cannot be expected that a draughtsman will make a good sketch for an article unless he knows what he is trying to draw. The object should be as clearly defined in the mind as if the completed work was before him; otherwise his drawing will be vague and uncertain.

As the purpose of the sketch is to show someone, usually a person ignorant of conventional methods of draughtsmanship, the appearance of the completed furniture, too much care cannot be taken in making the sketch accurate and showing the detail in a way that will leave little doubt in the mind what is intended, that there may be no cause for dissatisfaction with the completed article because the drawing was not understood.

The sketch should represent the article correctly, and sufficient skill to make such a drawing is obtained by practice. There is no better preparation for designing than drawing from existing examples of good furniture. By sitting in front of a chair, for instance, and drawing it as it appears, a knowledge of the way its curves and lines should be represented in a sketch are learned. It should be drawn as it is seen, not as it is known to be; that is, if the curve of the arm looks like a straight line, draw it so. If it is necessary that the curve appear on the sketch, change the position of the object so as to present the line as it is wanted, but do not make the drawing incorrect for the sake of presentation. A position can easily be taken that will show all that is necessary. If one drawing does not suffice to do so, make others rather than draw incorrectly.

The completed sketch should be as perfect a picture of the article as the draughtsman can make it in the time available. This is preferably a perspective drawing, though not necessarily one constructed mechanically. In fact, a free-hand drawing, made without the use of the conventional scales, is better. Of course, a knowledge of the principles and rules for making mechanical perspective is necessary to draw in this way, and if this knowledge is applied as the drawing proceeds the result will be satisfactory.

The object may be drawn of any convenient size and in a position that represents it to the best advantage. Certain articles may be drawn larger than others, and yet appear relatively of the proper dimensions. For instance, a chair may be drawn quite large to show all its details; while a cabinet is better sketched at a smaller scale, as otherwise it appears too large.

It is curious that to the uninitiated a large drawing or photograph represents a large object, and vice versa a small drawing a small object. So, when a light, delicate piece of furniture is to be represented the sketch should be small and delicately drawn.

Chairs look well drawn so the front is at an angle of about 45 degrees to the picture plane and with the corner nearest to the eye at a scale of one and a half inches to the foot.

It is not to be expected that a draughtsman can always have his ideas sufficiently formulated to enable him to draw a picture at once. Some preliminary work is required. A scale study may be made in orthographic projection to determine the proportion of the whole and the arrangement of the parts, and occasionally rough, full size drawings of parts requiring special study are made.

These projection drawings may be of any convenient scale, but most draughtsmen use one inch or one and one-half inch to the foot. With drawings made at these scales before him, the draughtsman has little difficulty in making his sketch correctly.

As any design becomes more attractive by a neat presentation, it is well to make first a study of the sketch with pencil, obtaining the general proportions and outline. Then, to save the time of making erasures and corrections, lay a piece of tracing paper over this rough study and make a more careful drawing. Repeat the process of making tracing copies, correcting the drawing each time until a satisfactory sketch is obtained. This may then be transferred to bristol board for the final rendering, or the last tracing copy is mounted and used as the final sketch. This is, indeed, a good way to do.

It is advisable to keep the rough studies, tracings and notes made when working up a design, either by pasting in scrap-books or

PLATE XXI.

PEN AND INK SKETCH OF A LOUIS XV. CHAIR.

classifying in portfolios. They will often be found convenient for duplicating sketches, suggesting ideas, etc.

The mediums and methods of rendering the final sketch are dependent on the personality of the draughtsman. The materials used by one designer might not please another, and each may have a different way of presenting the same object. Certain methods have been used by the best men, and seem to give satisfactory results, but someone may rightfully claim that other ways are equally as good.

The student can study the advantages and disadvantages of the leading methods and choose the one best suited to himself.

The lead pencil is an exceedingly pleasant medium for furniture sketching when used on a smooth, soft card, like ordinary mounting board. The point should not be too sharp, and with pencils of different degrees of hardness any amount of elaboration may be given the sketch. It may be delicately drawn in outline or it may be bold, broad and shaded if desired. Pen and ink are perhaps the best instruments for a clear indication of the facts. They are used by the majority of designers of experience, and many seem to prefer them to any other mediums. The inks available are the liquid India inks, Prout's brown, and writing fluids.

India ink has the advantage of giving a solid black line that does not change and that may be photographed for reproduction readily. It has the objection of being thick and of making an intensely black line, sometimes too heavy on smooth paper, unless a fine pen is used.

Prout's brown ink is not as intense in color as India ink, but it requires the proper combination of pen and paper to give the fine, delicate line best suited to furniture work.

Writing fluid, when used with a smooth surface writing paper and a moderately fine pen, gives very pleasing results. It flows readily, produces a fine line without the use of an exceedingly fine pen, and though not black when first used, it turns shortly after. The paper should be selected according to the ink and pen used; rough paper requires a coarse pen, and vice versa. Bristol board, India ink and a Gillot 303 pen make a good combination.

Sketches may be made in color, but this medium sometimes makes the furniture appear clumsy and uninteresting. The amount of small detail necessary to make a sketch serviceable is lost in a water color if it is broadly done, and if it is otherwise the drawing requires considerable time in rendering, besides seeming hard and mechanical. Water color is an excellent medium, however, for sketches of upholstered work. It enables the draughtsman to show the color of the goods, the pattern, and also to indicate the tufting with the least labor. Occasionally a combination of line drawing and color is serviceable, but it requires judicious handling, or the result is anything but artistic.

The purchaser of furniture is sometimes at a loss to know how much is necessary to furnish a room comfortably, and he can be advised most readily by the designer if a plan of the room is made and on it the furniture is laid out at scale. A convenient scale is one-half inch to the foot.

INDEX

Publications by Algrove Publishing Limited

The following is a list of titles from our popular *"Classic Reprint Series"* as well as a list of other publications by *Algrove Publishing Limited.*

Classic Reprint Series

Item #	Title
49L8024	☐ 1800 MECHANICAL MOVEMENTS AND DEVICES
49L8055	☐ 970 MECHANICAL APPLIANCES AND NOVELTIES OF CONSTRUCTION
49L8038	☐ A BOOK OF ALPHABETS WITH PLAIN, ORNAMENTAL, ANCIENT AND MEDIAEVAL STYLES
49L8074	☐ ARE YOU A GENIUS? WHAT IS YOUR I.Q?
49L8101	☐ ARTS-CRAFTS LAMPS & SHADES – *HOW TO MAKE THEM*
49L8016	☐ BARN PLANS & OUTBUILDINGS
49L8046	☐ BEAUTIFYING THE HOME GROUNDS
49L8014	☐ BOOK OF TRADES
49L8004	☐ BOULTON & PAUL, LTD. 1898 CATALOGUE
49L8012	☐ BOY CRAFT
49L8077	☐ CAMP COOKERY
49L8082	☐ CANADIAN WILD FLOWERS
49L8072	☐ CLASSIC PUZZLES AND HOW TO SOLVE THEM
49L8048	☐ CLAY MODELLING AND PLASTER CASTING
49L8005	☐ COLONIAL FURNITURE
49L8065	☐ COPING SAW WORK
49L8032	☐ DECORATIVE CARVING, PYROGRAPHY AND FLEMISH CARVING
49L8086	☐ FARM BLACKSMITHING
49L8031	☐ FARM MECHANICS
49L8029	☐ FARM WEEDS OF CANADA
49L8015	☐ FENCES, GATES & BRIDGES
49L8056	☐ FLORA'S LEXICON
49L8087	☐ FORGING
49L8706	☐ FROM LOG TO LOG HOUSE
49L8049	☐ HANDBOOK OF TURNING
49L8027	☐ HANDY FARM DEVICES AND HOW TO MAKE THEM
49L0720	☐ HOMES & INTERIORS OF THE 1920'S
49L8002	☐ HOW TO PAINT SIGNS & SHO' CARDS
49L8054	☐ HOW TO USE THE STEEL SQUARE
49L8001	☐ LEE'S PRICELESS RECIPES
49L8078	☐ MANUAL OF SEAMANSHIP FOR BOYS AND SEAMEN OF THE ROYAL NAVY, 1904
49L8020	☐ MISSION FURNITURE, HOW TO MAKE IT
49L8081	☐ MR. PUNCH WITH ROD AND GUN – *THE HUMOUR OF FISHING AND SHOOTING*
49L8073	☐ NAME IT! THE PICTORIAL QUIZ BOOK
49L8033	☐ ORNAMENTAL AND DECORATIVE WOOD CARVINGS
49L8089	☐ OVERSHOT WATER WHEELS FOR SMALL STREAMS
49L8059	☐ PROJECTS FOR WOODWORK TRAINING
49L8705	☐ REFLECTIONS ON THE FUNGALOIDS
49L8003	☐ RUSTIC CARPENTRY
49L8044	☐ SAM LOYD'S PICTURE PUZZLES
49L8030	☐ SHELTERS, SHACKS & SHANTIES
49L8085	☐ SKELETON LEAVES AND PHANTOM FLOWERS
49L8068	☐ SPECIALIZED JOINERY
49L8052	☐ STANLEY COMBINATION PLANES – *THE 45, THE 50 & THE 55*
49L8050	☐ STRONG'S BOOK OF DESIGNS
49L8064	☐ THE ARCHITECTURE OF COUNTRY HOUSES
49L8034	☐ THE ART OF WHITTLING
49L8018	☐ THE BOY'S BOOK OF MECHANICAL MODELS
49L8071	☐ THE BULL OF THE WOODS, VOL.1
49L8080	☐ THE BULL OF THE WOODS, VOL.2
45L0106	☐ THE DUCHESS OF BLOOMSBURY STREET
49L8021	☐ THE INTERNATIONAL CYCLOPEDIA OF MONOGRAMS
49L8053	☐ THE METALWORKING LATHE
49L8023	☐ THE OPEN TIMBER ROOFS OF THE MIDDLE AGES
49L8076	☐ THE WILDFLOWERS OF AMERICA
49L8057	☐ THE WILDFLOWERS OF CANADA
49L8058	☐ THE YANKEE WHALER
49L8025	☐ THE YOUNG SEA OFFICER'S SHEET ANCHOR
49L8047	☐ TIMBER – *FROM THE FOREST, TO ITS USE IN COMMERCE*
49L8061	☐ TRADITIONS OF THE NAVY
49L8042	☐ TURNING FOR AMATEURS
49L8039	☐ VIOLIN MAKING AS IT WAS, AND IS
49L8079	☐ WILLIAM BULLOCK & CO. – *HARDWARE CATALOG, CIRCA 1850*
49L8019	☐ WINDMILLS AND WIND MOTORS
49L8013	☐ YOU CAN MAKE IT
49L8035	☐ YOU CAN MAKE IT FOR CAMP & COTTAGE
49L8036	☐ YOU CAN MAKE IT FOR PROFIT

Other Algrove Publications

Item #	Title
49L8601	☐ ALL THE KNOTS YOU NEED
49L8707	☐ BUILDING THE NORWEGIAN SAILING PRAM (MANUAL AND PLANS)
49L8708	☐ BUILDING THE SEA URCHIN (MANUAL AND PLANS)
49L8084	☐ THE ART OF ARTHUR WATTS
49L8067	☐ WOOD HANDBOOK – *WOOD AS AN ENGINEERING MATERIAL*
49L8060	☐ WOODEN PLANES AND HOW TO MAKE THEM